i

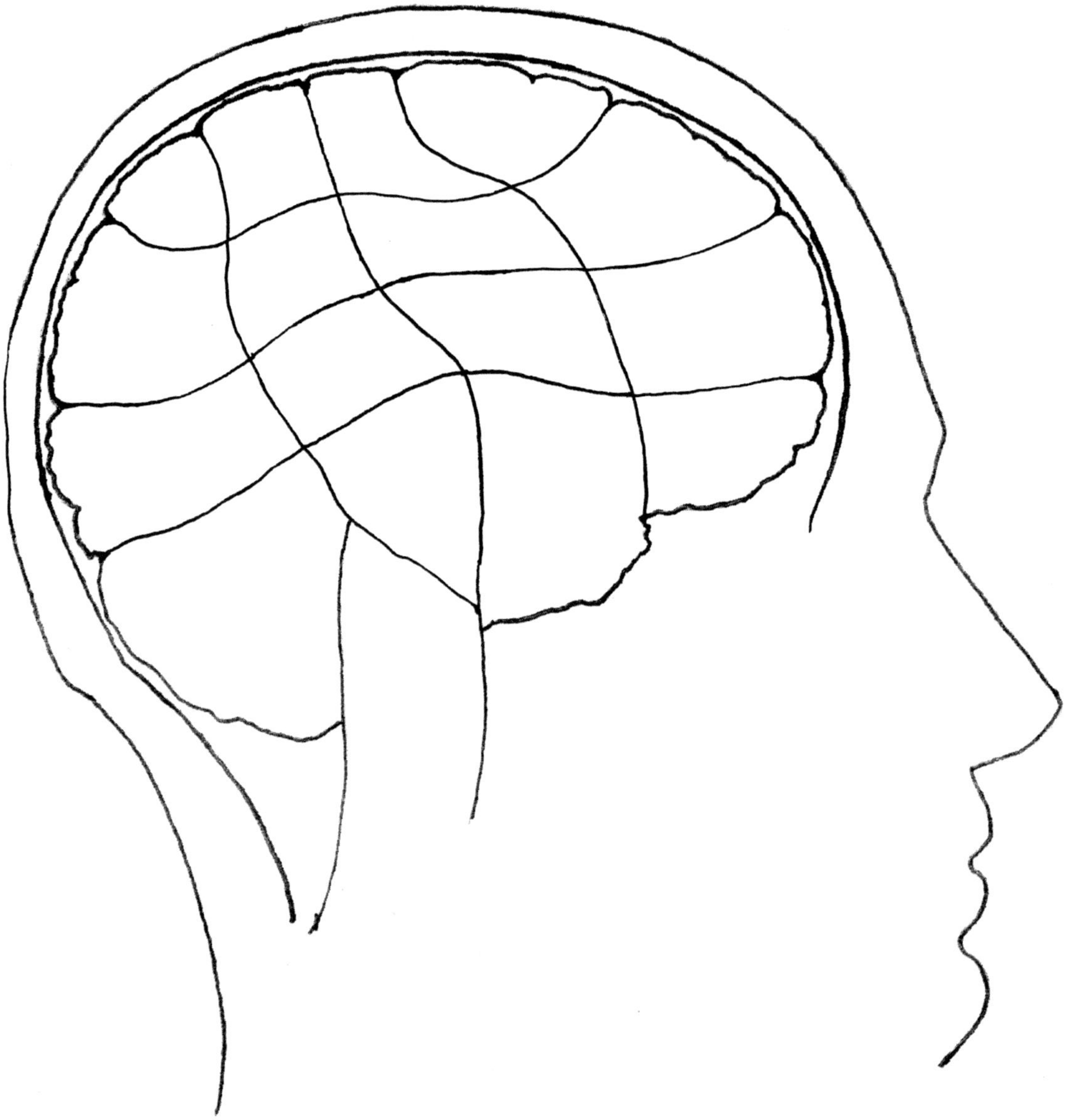

GENR8

TECHNOLOGY GROUP INC.

Signs & Symbols of Success
Branding Manual including
The Matriarchy of Brands Edition
Copyright © 2019 by Bryce Maynard Winter
First Edition Volume One in the Scents of Success Series
by The Media Lab Vancouver
ISBN: 9781796782509
Scents of Success Series is published by The Media Lab
division of GENR8 Technology Group Inc.
Vancouver,
Canada

SCENTS OF
SUCCESS
SERIES

Signs &
Symbols
of Success

Learn how branding TRULY works.

Benefit from my experience with 100s of clients
and brands from Evian to Virgin, to generate:

- *Increasing product or service demand "automagically"*
- *Higher revenues & gross margins = more and greater profits*
- *Better budgets—including for clients, brands & your salary!*

Whether you are a Student, an Artist, an Entrepreneur, Brand Manager, College Director, Designer, Art Director or Story Developer, *Signs & Symbols of Success* is your guide to clarity and certainty in developing, building and executing better brand strategies and effective messages.

NOT a one-size-fits all solution, *Signs & Symbols of Success* is actually a guidebook to proven best-practices for any situation, demonstrated by all persistent winners of *Interbrand's Best Global Brands* (the top 100 brands are assessed and rated annually by the world's largest brand agency).

Learn how to develop positive qualities of many of the great brands I have worked with, from CHANEL to Timberland, Virgin, & even Government!

You will experience:

7 Secrets to Brand Anything
- ☑ How to NAIL your brand's conversational flavor
- ☑ Get how your competition works better than they do
- ☑ How branding is actually generated

Matriarchy of Brands:
- ☑ Formulae for every brand including colors, flavors
- ☑ Strategic insight into contemporaneous profit formulas
- ☑ Why branding is neither as complicated, nor likely as simple as you think

Branding for Profit:
- ☑ How unspoken promises differentiate brands
- ☑ The psychology at play and how it actually connects
- ☑ The most efficient and effective means to spread rapidly

Scents of Success:
- ☑ Parties, stores, stories and examples
- ☑ Entry points to the world of branding
- ☑ Frames to help your thinking about your messaging

Dedication

For Aurora.

Thanks

To all my family, the best of the best!

Event conceived by the author in art above; followed by the live event, featuring Lena Love, below.

Signs & Symbols of Success

BRANDING MANUAL

introducing for the first time in print

THE MATRIARCHY OF BRANDS

I love words: THERE *I said it*. Why? Perhaps I have found that words have meaning beyond what you might think or feel or seems obvious.

Words capture energy, which when *aspirated** (to pronounce a sound with exhalation of breath)
are released with an explosive, *catalytic quality* (acts as a substance that increases the rate of a reaction without itself undergoing any permanent change)
to *all and sundry** (everyone in all shapes and sizes).

Words ignite ideas, illuminate concepts and bring fire to movements.

Words move, delight and transfix us.
Words communicate powerfully.

Words are important. This is a book, in many ways, about words. Just that the words we are talking about describe ideas, forms and colors as well as other rational ideas in a simple, easy structure that anyone can learn. With sufficient practice, you may even become an expert. If you are already an expert, prepare to be upgraded: the information contained in this compact volume has never before been made widely available. *It has been a secret.*

You too can develop the qualities of a top-100 global brand by learning how to:

- Communicate on **conscious** and **unconscious** levels
- **Invite licensing,** plus residual sales opportunities and systems
- Become **harmonious** (makes sense and look/sound/smell right)

Understand the Real Purpose of Brand Design is to create a Residual Effect, like Ringing a Bell!

Color: Communicate clearly and efficiently by directly accessing emotion with the right color palette, a fundamental lever of any real brand.

Charisma based on Character: Your brand has a personality and a character that is essential to your success. Find a fool-proof recipe for discovering brand character, and charisma.

Conversation(s): Your brand personality has a life of its own; real brands are carried on the cultural conversations of others. Through effective use of this little book, you will be able to promote residuality, and:

1. Reduce friction through familiarity and real customer ease
2. Become more and more familiar and stay familiar with people
3. Be the favored product/service in your category/niche

This virtuous cycle is exhibited by all successful brand designs.

Here, in this slim volume, is how you can too!

*Understand that I am an *etymologist*. No, this is *not* somebody with an interest in insects. This is someone with an interest in words, where they come from, and what their meanings are; hidden and otherwise, as well.

Forward

In Signs & Symbols of Success I hope to have produced a volume on professional branding that would have meaningfully helped me out, twenty-eight years ago, when I first started doing "branding" work, as a foundational reference to build experience on.

Because there was no central authority at the time, I took to whatever books or people of influence I could find. From marketing books on writing direct sales copy to advertising books on headlines and layout to conversations with the window dresser, I was a sponge. But, like you, I had other things to do as well, namely in my case running a store, getting more sales and starting a desktop design and pre-print agency.

Since then, through a career in branding crossing everything from promotion of cigarettes to large-scale government sector employee engagement programs and strategy for fashion houses, for fund-raisers and for fun, I have found a consistent handful of patterns and rules that, once distinguished, together provide a 'codex' that explains the strategy of brand behavior *every time*.

Everyone at some points struggles to get it all working and tries to make sense of it all. That is why direct sales companies like Amway or Mary Kay and franchises like Subway and Jiffy Lube thrive. These companies (to differing levels of success) have happened on many of the 'secrets' in this book and sorted out how to apply them to an empire. As a franchisee you just 'add water and mix', then 'bake in a preheated oven at 350 degrees for 10-12 minutes' and presto, professional brand (that's the theory, anyhow).

The thing is, not all of us want to be part of an existing brand mixture, nor do we wish to apply the limits of the past embedded in these formulas. Some of us want to build better businesses, launch larger movements, start smarter empires, create bigger best-sellers and change the world for the freer. If you are such a person, this book is for you!

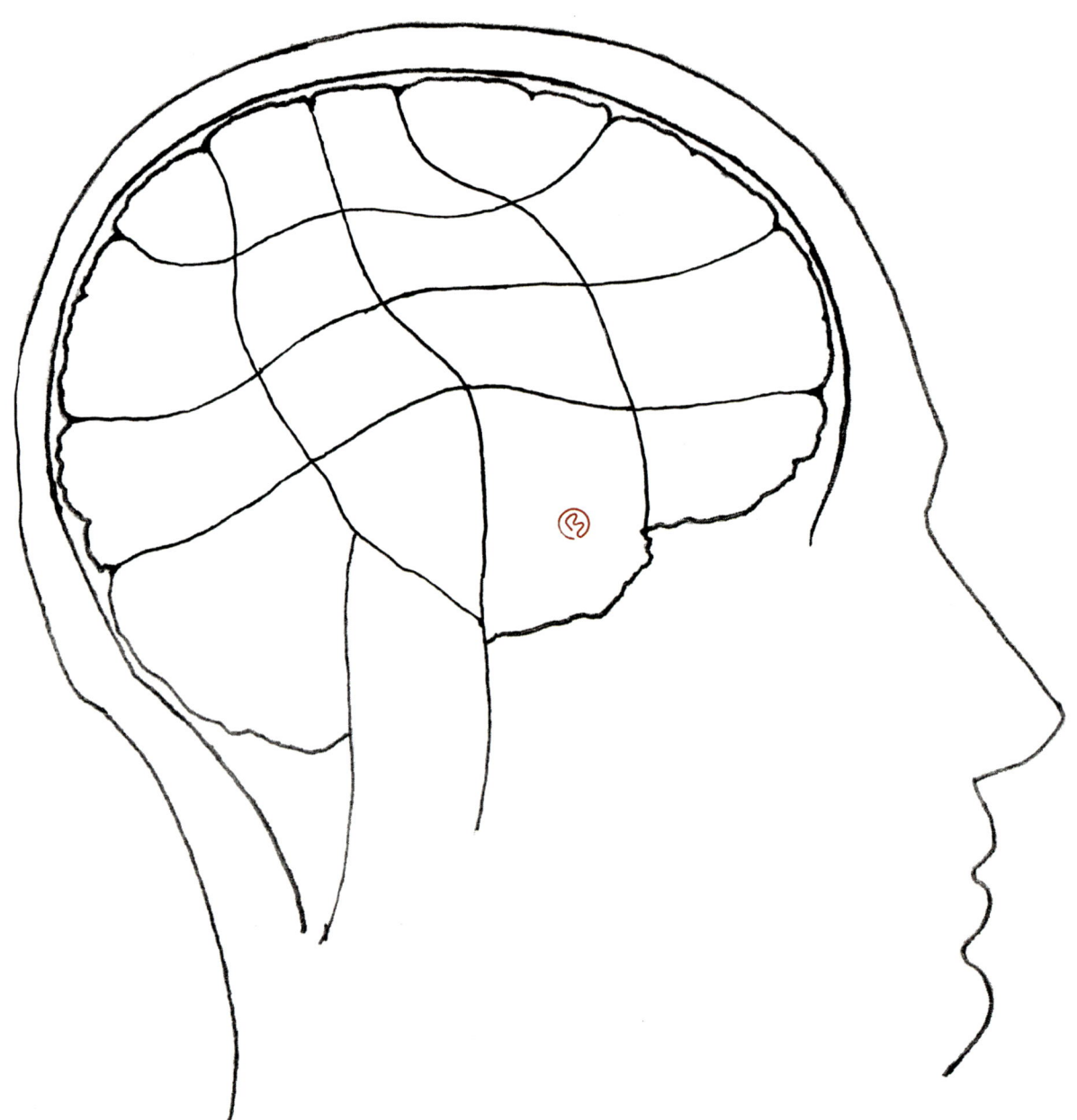

Contents

Introduction

Branding often occurs around a series of pivotal moments. Moments of 'high impression' which force themselves on our consciousness such that they leave a mark: should I say marque?

Moments are by definition surprising and full of clarity that cannot be imagined earlier if you were to try. My most famous branding moment, as a child, was being able to recognize the make and model of on-coming cars through their headlight design at a distance, while travelling at night in the centre seat of our family's Oldsmobile Delta 88 Custom Royale. Earlier it as the centre seat of our 1963 Chrysler New Yorker, like the one seen below.

The cars seen through the windshields of these chariots had names like Beetle (or Bug), Cadillac, Lincoln, Mercedes and Mercury, occasionally something a little rare or stranger would come along, like a Corvette, or a Corvair or maybe even a Rolls-Royce. There was a special rule: if one of the headlights was burnt out in the oncoming car, then call out "Donkey!" and sister and her boyfriend could kiss!

As an all-time winner in the correct identification of car brands at a distance awards, I found some renown in being able to articulate the differences in said forms. For instance, I found that both Chrysler and Volkswagen had smiling 'happy' faces while Ford and its divisions had wide square toothy grins. The Mercedes of the late 60s and early 70s to me had large furrowed brows of headlights with hulking huge grill spaced in between, much like the even more upright and large Rolls-Royce, except it had much closer more feminine wider and curvy brow than the German car.

Whether the signs and symbols of success for your brand, project, idea, company or client evolve from the shape of headlights and radiator grills, or, more likely, from an e-experience of some kind evolving into an inner experience, this is a book on what and how to look for the signs & symbols of success when it comes to written-convertible communication.

What are the signs and symbols of success? Traditionally, in our economy, many people identify signs and symbols of success with things like rich clothing, vehicles, houses and vacations.

Is that what I mean? Yes, and no. Yes, insofar as many of these things are products of branding. No, because the signs and symbols of success we are talking about are the subtle (and not so subtle) ways that well-constructed, effective brands employ on a daily basis around the world, *driving and directing* most of the discretionary income in our economy.

What is branding? Branding is the practice of applying communication principles and ideas to a company, product, or group in such a way people 'get it' in a hurry. Professional branding makes complex things easily understandable and accessible through ordinary language.

The language of professional branding includes:

- Correct color
- Fundamental form (including shape and gender)
- Subtle scent and other direct communications means including order, name, and vocabulary, as well as the power of veto, to stake its claim
- Congruent strategy: aligns all moving parts of brand, media, message

Therefore, this book is truly about applying all forms of media to your company, product, group or project in a way that others may understand your underlying and overarching premise; and promise.

Amazing how talking about communications takes so many words! That is why brands are so important. Brands present complex messages easily in ways that saves words, saves time, and (theoretically, at least!) saves paper.

This volume is divided into FOUR main parts:

1. 7 SECRETS TO BRANDING ANYTHING
2. THE MATRIARCHY OF BRANDS
3. BRANDING FOR PROFIT
4. SCENTS OF SUCCESS

Each section has a different emphasis and at different times will be what you want. You may also find that a second read reveals completely new realizations you had not seen or connected before. This is because it is not until you have read it all that conscious connections become real and obvious

Section one, *7 Secrets to Branding Anything*, is the logic; or brains, of this book.

Section two, *The Matriarchy of Brands*, is the heart of this book. For the first time in print, and all together in one place, you will find the holy grail of branding, a singular and straightforward family of 'archetypes' in which is represented the specific color form and brand behavior of every single sustained top brand. The magic of this section is its comprehensive nature within a simple structure that allows you to see both big picture and details at a glance. You may never look at brands the same way again, after completing this section.

In *Branding for Profit*, we apply many of the principles and lessons of *7 Secrets to Branding* and *The Matriarchy of Brands* through stories and articles that serve to further expand dominion of this work. You will see how Professional Branding is an applied skillset that enhances value and provides superior leverage in business and organization in a wide variety of ways beyond mere sales and marketing, and that, very well, also!

By the time you get to finding your *Scents of Success*, it is my belief that you will be able to view brand strategy as a reliable, stable and valuable piece of business strategy for almost any kind of organization, from start-up to Fortune 500, including not-for-profits, government, new economy and more, *and* have a good understanding of many of the right elements to focus on and how.

Prepare to learn how and why it is that:

- A handful of fairytales control most of the world's economies
- Misuse of green is a (major) cause of the failure of Eco movements
- It is what you DON'T say, NOT what you DO that matters most
- You may be able to cash in too, if you can learn the rules in time
- Performing to the letter and the spirit is essential in all cases
- Actions speak (much) louder than words
- Matriarchy is in branding's nature

This book is a survey course in brand standards and components that is designed to provide user-accessible information on how brands work in a deconstructed way for the people who run them, so they may be able to do more effective jobs, improve communication efficiency and decrease loss or slippage due to missed opportunity, error or confused or mixed messages.

Success Factors, the Signs & Symbols of Success

I have chosen to focus on identifying the top eight essential qualities relating to consistency and success. Read the following left to right.

#	Adjective	Noun	Essential Quality
I	Conscious	Color	Hue
II	Failsafe	Form	Shape
III	Curious	Question	Brand
IIII	Alternative	Answer	Elevator
V	Archetypal	Archetype	Persona
VI	Successful	Scent	Truth
VII	Perfect	Promise	Secret
VIII	Trustworthy	Texture	Architecture

Together, this set of success factors in turn relates specifically to the behavior of each and every sort of brand, each of which is documented, with popular and easy-to-understand examples, in this book.

What ARE the Signs & Symbols of Success? When I set out to write this book, at first, I thought it was all about releasing and granting some hidden powers of the economy to a wider audience. As it progressed, however, I came to see the contents of this book as both symbolic and also "signallic", a made-up word by which I mean catalytic in sending a signal. By taking form in shape, color and mood, or design; the signs and symbols of success discussed in this book as readily access emotion, as a compass finds direction.

Maybe that is what the Signs & Symbols of Success are *really* all about: predictability. We all want to have a treasure map, we need to understand what are the buttons and levers we must push and pull to impact our audience and get our message across. This, for the first time, is it.

Knowing, and understanding the Signs & Symbols of Success may change your life forever. I clearly recall when the final puzzle pieces were dropping into place that I suddenly saw so clearly the need for every brand—and exactly how they all fit together. Almost as quickly, I began to see which brands were off—and how, precisely, to fix them all, from small to large.

The whole world is evolving and shifting very quickly and many of the ways it is changing immediately impact you and affect your brand. From media consolidation, to interactive social media, the rules for promotion and marketing are changing every day. But archetypes, and therefore the character of brands, are by their very nature unchanging. Knowing and understanding your brand's archetype is a long-term investment in the equity of your business and will pay back handsome dividends.

Brands frequently operate on the level of what is unstated and unsaid, leveraging the power of the unstated to become pervasive in their message, while actually saying nothing direct at all!

What brands do communicate, however, is a long list of the signs and symbols of success, from colors to logos to slogans. In this book we capture and systematize all of these key signs and symbols and classify them.

Use this book to promote and develop your effectiveness and consistency while working on:

- Captions, cartoons, drawings, illustrations, names, slogans, titles
- Brochures, websites and other digital assets
- Employee loyalty programs
- Contract development
- Product development
- Marketing programs
- Marketing strategy
- Creative sessions
- Proposal writing
- Documentation
- Brainstorming
- Sales tactics
- Media kits
- Sales copy
- Brands
- Logos

Use the architectural metaphors and persona structures to focus brainstorm sessions into targeted creative sessions, while developing a narrative for new projects and breathing new life into core messaging for your organization.

Application of this content may impact and improve all kinds of crucial interstitial and end-goals connected to communications, including

- Making money
- Recording ideas
- Building connections
- Creating relationships
- Arrangements of things
- Getting things into order

I would love to hear and see your success story, how you were able to see a new breakthrough? Send your 30–60-second clip or art to success@genr8.me

I look forward to seeing and hearing your story!

Bryce Maynard Winter
Brand Architect, Producer of Automagical Excellence
The Media Lab c/o GENR8 Technology Group Inc.
CANADA

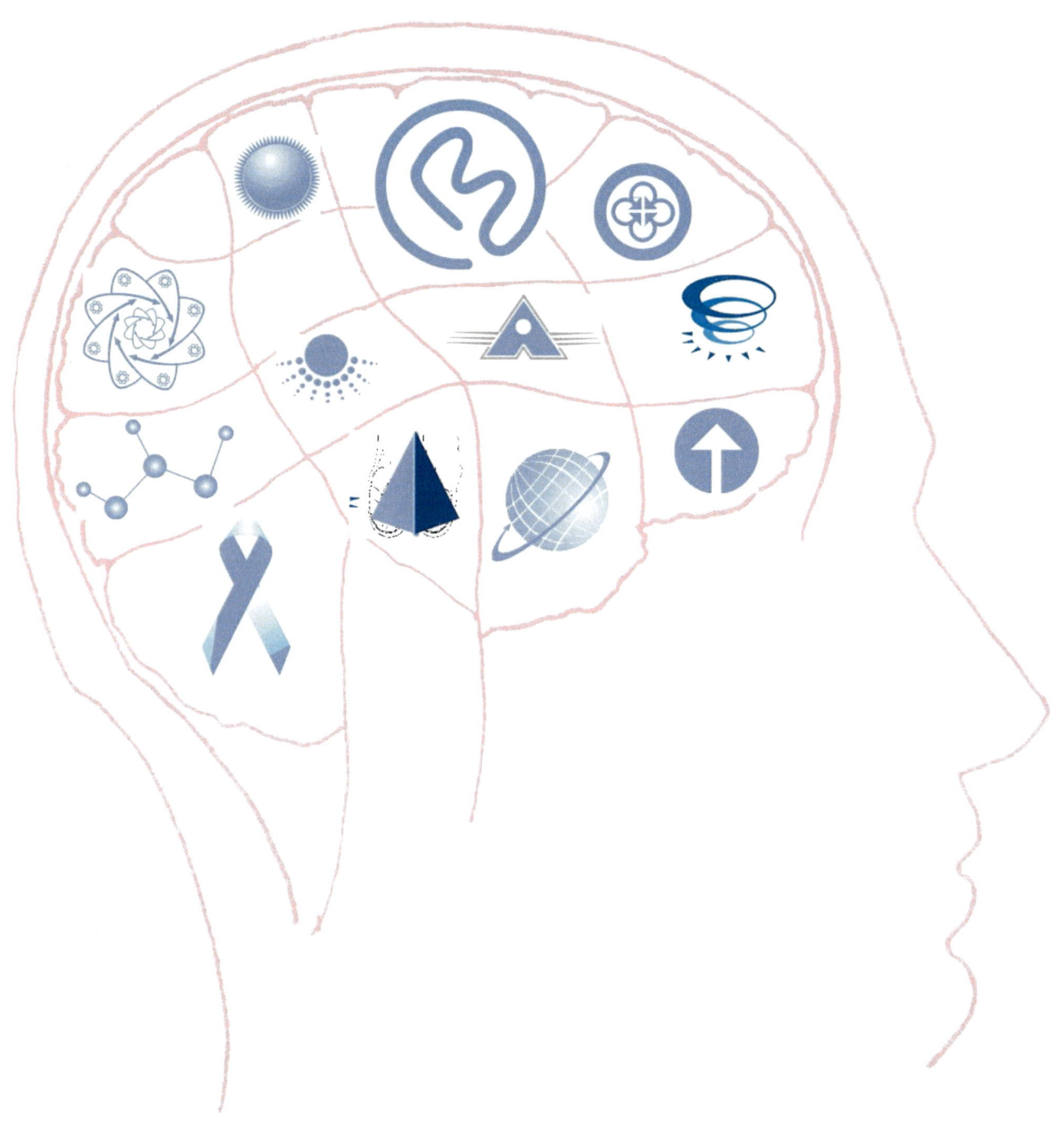

7 Secrets
to Branding
Anything

Synopsis: 7 Secrets to Branding Anything, listed.

1. *A brand is a story.* Period.
2. The *story exists in minds of customers* —not managers.
3. *You didn't invent the story & neither did your customers!*
4. *Stick to the story.* "That's my story, and I'm sticking to it."
5. *Believe* in the story.
6. The *stories are just fairy tales* (true lies).
7. There are only *seven key stories,* your job is to identify one story and fine-tune it.

You know how riding a bicycle seems so easy, once you've done it, but learning involves a lot of wobbly moments, and frequently more than a few scraped knees? Learning and understanding how branding really works is a bit like that. Once you can clearly see how brands and branding work, your vision of the world will never be the same again. And just like riding a bicycle, once you learn how; you will never forget!

Understanding what is an archetype is one the first elements in this story:

ar·che·type

/ˈärkəˌtīp/ ◀)

noun
noun: **archetype**; plural noun: **archetypes**

a very typical example of a certain person or thing.
"the book is a perfect archetype of the genre"

- an original that has been imitated.
"the archetype of faith is Abraham"
synonyms: quintessence, essence, representative, model, embodiment, prototype, stereotype;
More

- a recurrent symbol or motif in literature, art, or mythology.
"mythological archetypes of good and evil"

- PSYCHOANALYSIS
(in Jungian psychology) a primitive mental image inherited from the earliest human ancestors, and supposed to be present in the collective unconscious.

A system that we use is based on the architectural metaphor that existing terminology is based on. Terms like 'House Brand' and 'Bridge Brand' have been around for decades. In this book we introduce a complete and consistent series of architectural terms for all brands. We call this new set of terms, based on architectural metaphor and reference, Architectonics. Webster defines architectonics as the "unifying structural design of something, and also the system of structure". Architectonics as a language reference system refers to both of these aspects. Through the brand language of Architectonics, we define the unifying features of each brand formula and also a greater system to refer to different brand aspects within each type or kind. CROMA is one such application I have developed.

Using CROMA it is possible to develop symphonies of color messaging, communicating through palette unconsciously entire message series.

Understanding why we use an architectural metaphor is relevant if working within the built environment. Otherwise, it may simply be relevant to understand that the human world is constructed like a built environment—as are brands—and that this is the most basic and easy basis form of metaphor. By using this metaphor we are able to decipher shapes, forms, color and messages.

Architectonics

The master brand formulae work within a seven-point catechism, following:

1. *A brand is a story.* **Period.**
2. **The** *story exists in minds of customers* **—not managers.**
3. *You didn't invent the story & neither did your customers!*
4. *Stick to the story.* **"That's my story, and I'm sticking to it."**
5. *Believe* **in the story.**
6. **The** *stories are just fairy tales* **(true lies).**
7. **There are only** *seven key stories,* **your job is to identify one and fine-tune it.**

This is actually quite exciting news! It means that we can quite easily develop a roadmap to success for your brand. The 'heavy lifting' has already been done by those ahead of us: the hundreds of long-standing and successful brands that have worked out, through trial and error, what works, and most importantly, what does not. The top 100 brands are exhaustively reviewed and analyzed on an annual basis by Interbrand, the New York-based International Branding Agency.

'Like the *Billboard 100*, the *Interbrand 100* is based on actual sales and market-share results of thousands of companies. Analyzing the *Interbrand 100* year to year is like seeing our culture in a mirror. We can see both what works (rising brands) and what does not (falling or failing brands). Plus, most of the companies on the *Interbrand 100* are publicly-traded companies, so there is significant and impartial financial information available on them. Our work has for years involved analyzing these companies, trends and searching for similarities in strategy, scope and understanding.

We call these the tenets of Architectonics, through which we can architect, engineer, design and build better brands at will.

Secret 1. A brand is a story

While technically we define a brand as: *the set of relationships through which a commercial, organizational or product identity connects with people;* in practice we simply state: "A brand is a story." Fundamentally the set of relationships through which an identity connects with people is through stories. More formally, it is *a* story—the story is that of the brand's hero.

Consistency makes a brand great; consistency is required to produce a brand at all. The question is, consistent with what? You will hear a thousand answers from anything like color and font to price, policy and communication method. The truth is ALL of these may be important yet none is as pervasive as story.

Story is a shortcut to memory, emotion and what would otherwise be chaotic assemblages of words, meaning and messages that all combine instantly in some kind of order through the magic of story: think of this.

Rapunzel

Long, long ago in a house that overlooked a beautiful garden lived a childless couple. They prayed every day to bless them with a child. One day they found prayers had been answered. They were at long last going to have a baby!

Their days passed in happiness but alas! the wife fell ill. She would eat nothing and the husband was worried that she would waste away. He tried to tempt her with many good things but she refused everything. "But you must eat something, my dear," he begged her. "There is a herb called Rapunzel in the garden next door. I will feel better if I can eat that," she said. The husband's heart sank when he heard her. This garden was owned by a wicked witch who would let no one enter. But he loved his wife very much and so with a pounding heart, he decided to go into the garden at a time when the witch was away. One day, finding an appropriate time he went into the garden. He had managed to pluck the herb but as he was about to leave, the wicked witch came back. "You thief! How dare you enter my garden?" she screamed. She threatened to put a curse on him. He fell at her feet and begged, "Please don't curse me. If my wife doesn't eat this herb, she will die. She is going to have a baby and is very ill." The witch stopped to think awhile. "I will let you go on one condition. You will give me the baby after it's born." The poor man had no other way out but to agree.

He took the herb to his wife and miraculously she soon recovered and gave birth to a beautiful girl. But as per the agreement the witch came to take the baby away. She took Rapunzel—for that's what she named her—far away and locked her in a high tower. The tower had no doors or stairs. There was only a window on top.

The only person whom Rapunzel ever saw was the wicked witch. Rapunzel grew up to become beautiful with pretty eyes, a beautiful voice, and her golden hair grew very, very long. All day long, when Rapunzel was alone, she would sing and weep.

Every day, the wicked witch came to the tower with food. She stood at the bottom of the tower and shouted. "Rapunzel! Rapunzel! Let your hair down!" Rapunzel would drop her long, braided hair through the window. The witch used the hair as a rope to climb into the tower.

One day, a handsome prince was passing by and heard her sing. He fell in love with her voice and unknown to all came to the tower every day to hear her sing. One day, the prince saw the witch climbing up the tower using Rapunzel's hair.

The next day, the prince too called out to Rapunzel. "Let down your hair," he said. The prince climbed to the top of the tower. After that, the prince came to meet Rapunzel every night.

Alas! the witch soon discovered the prince with Rapunzel. She pushed him from the tower onto a thorny bush, making him blind. She banished Rapunzel into the desert far away.

This is the first of several original illustrations directed by the author. While this figure was commissioned earlier and is not necessarily of Rapunzel, it is lovely and does convey a textured and detailed domestic atmosphere of private femininity ..perhaps this is Rapunzel at home.

Many years passed. The blind prince wandered alone and finally reached the same desert. One day, he heard familiar voice singing. Following the sound, he found her. They hugged each other in joy. Tears of happiness rolled down Rapunzel's cheek. As the tears fell on the prince's eyes, he regained his vision.

The prince took Rapunzel to his kingdom and they lived happily ever after!

Discussion Questions:

Who was the victim in the story?

_____

Who was the villain?

_____

What was the hero?

_____

Rapunzel has magical properties.
What every day magic does she stand for?

_____

_____

What quality(ies) that Rapunzel longs for is something everyone wants?

_____

_____

What popular brand could be represented by the gist this story?

_____

_____

_____

What brand could be said to have Rapunzel's image as a brand logo?

_____

Secret 2. The story exists
in minds of customers—not sellers

The focus of the location of the story must remain with the public, not the brand owners. This reflects that while brand owners may have a vested interest in a particular outcome, or specific aspect of the story, the actual story that the public holds in its collective mind is the story that matters.

It seems obvious. The results produced by a play are judged by the audience, not the players, the playwright, the producer, the director or the decorator. So it is with brands. Whatever story your group thinks you are presenting is irrelevant to your audience, customers. The only story that matters to customers is the story they tell themselves.

This means, among things, that it is doubly important to be clear on what your story is, especially internally, so that all individuals, departments and divisions can deploy consistently across all channels. This is one more reason favoring stories, as they are archetypally memorable and therefore easy to calibrate across spectra—especially important in today's multimedia universe.

Knowing your brand's story in a short, snappy way unifies workforces, ties communications together and brings about harmony, quickly.

If you have ever been caught out with one person's understanding or assumption of your motive or actions not as you intended; then you know how important it is to be clearly understood. That is why brands can hardly overcommunicate once they are aligned. Only when falling from alignment or wobbling, like a spinning apple would does communication falter. This is because of fundamental misalignment with the underlying story, which as we said, yet bears repeating, exists primarily in the minds of your customer, not you, Mr./Ms. Brand Owner. That means, for shareholders of large household brand names, as you press brands out of integrity by putting short term profits ahead of viable brand equity; you squeeze opportunity from the long game, because someone else will pick up the torch in the gap left by the household brand name in its rush for short sales. This is what has been happening on a modest scale for a number of years, and has created both a proliferation and a concentration of brands, especially in media.

You do not have to be a newbie to make the mistake of believing what your business plan says is what truly is. Companies as large as Coca-Cola have made this a billion-dollar mistake, from time to time. The best way to find out what your story is to ask your customers what they think or feel.

Discussion Questions:

Where does brand story exist?

_____

Who writes a play, the playwright or the audience? Why? Why not?

_____

What's more important, the game or the fan experience?

_____

What is someone who makes up a story about you; then makes you the villain of the story they made up?

_____

What is someone who makes up a story about you and makes you the hero of the story?

_____

Do you think it is easy to shift brand stories? Why? Why not?

_____

What story already exists in the minds of customers that I can align with?

_____

_____

_____

_____

_____

Secret 3. You didn't invent the story & neither did your customers!

While brand owners may be credited with establishing certain aspects of the story, and members of the public can and should be credited with picking up the story, neither party actually invents the story. Instead, the story exists in the psychological Gestalt that is already present, even at the time prior to the establishment of the brand. This is a critical aspect to understand.

This one can be a mind-bender and I must admit that the subtlety of it eluded me for years, until I gained sufficient understanding in various seemingly esoteric topics like Jungian psychology as well as research and writings by practical philosophers like Canadian Marshall McLuhan and Noam Chomsky as well as a great understanding of human behavior and thought processes through hundreds of professional relationships.

Here is what you have to know. We are all 'programmed' with some pretty basic story-telling stuff from early one. We learn about the hero and our villain. We learn about the damsel and the knight. All of this information (and we each likely contain giga-quads of it by an early age) is actually pretty consistent from person to person and even across cultures.

When you talk about a Queen, I have an immediate understanding of a sort of personality, with differences from a Princess, for instance, in many notable ways. In actuality, however, there are a limited number of common stories we all understand, but those there are, are SO commonplace that everybody immediately understands your meaning. Catches your drift. Down with your jive. They get you.

So, with brands, it turns out the only stories that really work are these common ones. It makes sense, if you think about it, because brands really are pretty powerful and just about perform like magic, so it seems unlikely this is just because everybody working there is clever. No, it is something similar yet different. Everybody working there got luckily enough onto one of those core common stories and agreed on the direction and then everyone got hold of it and yay, they did not need to learn the story, just connect it with their version of this story they already had!

In simple terms, this is why brand loyalty exists. We are fond of our stories and so, subsequent harmonic brand associations are reassuring on quite a deep psychologic level.

Discussion Questions:

Where does story come from?

_____

Do you believe in dreams? Do you dream? Does everybody dream?

_____

Why do people tell stories?

_____

What is the first story you remember?

_____

Was it real or was it Disney?

_____

Do you tell stories to yourself? What about with others? Isn't life a story?

_____

What story elements do you know are in your brand?

_____

_____

_____

_____

_____

_____

_____

Secret 4. Stick to the story
"That's my story, and I'm sticking to it."

What really makes a brand story stick is the stick of its progenitors: those who start and establish the brand. Often, about the time a brand's founders are beginning to get really tired of a brand's story is also when the public is *beginning* to pick up on it. It is absolutely vital that you do not 'change horses' midstream. Doing so is anathema (opposing intention) to better branding, and one may as well start from scratch if that is one's approach.

Human nature being what it is and attention span being what *it* is (currently approaching that of a fruit fly, I hear), you are going to want to switch stories, or at least make major renovations to it.

Do not. At least not until further analysis.

Once you are able to identify your story and attune your organization to it, it may take some time for everyone to pick up on it. Remember, the story is not even yours, and mainly is in your customers' minds, not your managers.

So, all you can really do is sort of guide it, stick-handle it, gently and easily into a form or a goal that already exists. You can't change the goal and expect fans not to boo and hiss and likely leave the stadium.

To brand is a long game and requires resolution and commitment to a cause and a story. Revelation may return considerable interest in your investment towards consistency—after a while. Losses, however, can occur frequently and all too fatally for brands that do not maintain resolution with one steady story.

How many people recall the original 'smart' phone device, the Blackberry? Unfortunately for its maker, shareholders and customers, this brand was distracted by the launch of a competitive product, the Apple iPhone and became almost overnight 'second best'. In reality, Research In Motion's corporate strategy was never the same story as Apple's, yet Apple's superior ability to get its strong story across, combined with Blackberry's ongoing inability to clearly see their own story has created a dynamic which the role of the original 'smart' phone brand has become that of an almost irrelevant bit player.

Too many Canadian companies, in particular, from Blackberry to The Hudson's Bay Company to Eaton's to Woodward's, have shifted stories when the going got tough and deluded themselves into thinking they were adjusting to market conditions when they had in fact lost sight of their originating and powerful stories as leaders and became instead market followers, trailing downwards with ever-decreasing market share into oblivion.

If your story is sounding or seeming irrelevant, then it may be time to dig a little deeper into it, rather than just switching stories. Switching stories is anathema to brands, and usually makes about as much sense as setting fire to your customer lists.

It may be tempting, if occasional embarrassments arise, to apologize for your brand's character. Don't. Do not do that. If your brand is out of character, then apologize. If it is in character and someone does not like it, do not apologize. Thank them for their opinion and move on. They are not fans. It's okay for not everyone to like you. Actually, it is pretty much required that some people won't like your brand, if only to even out the number of people who LOVE it!

Stick to your story. If questioned, I have always felt it helpful to say with an affirmative nod: "That's my story, and I'm sticking to it!"

People like that.

It is okay to make a point. You will find that being boring is less valuable in the market than brands that have character—sticking to their story, even when or if parts of it seem unpopular. There is a good reason for your story that will surface.

Do not become a forgotten brand.

While the Bay is still around in Canada and most Canadians probably still think of it as Canadian, it is no longer the company listed above. HBC is now foreign-owned and controlled state-side.

Discussion Questions:

What do you think of politicians who forget their promises after elections?

_____

_____

What is the worst thing that can happen by 'sticking to your story'?

_____

What is the best thing that can happen by 'sticking to your story'?

_____

What character or story had the most influence on you as a child?

_____

_____

What character or story has the most influence on you now?

_____

_____

_____

What does it feel like to stick to your story?

_____

What is your story?

_____

_____

_____

Secret 5. Believe in the story

It's not enough to say the right words.

If you don't believe in what you are up to, you're sunk.

While a story may (by its very nature) be fiction; it is required, nay, *imperative,* that those behind the brand believe whole-heartedly in the story, anyway!

Just as it is anathema to change stories, it would be disingenuous to not believe in the story. This requires patience and understanding for founders, for others who are recruited into the brand may not at first understand or believe.

If you need an example, look no farther than Disneyland, the magic mountain of success in theme parks. While if you dig, or have worked for the theatrical behemoth you will easily know many of the secrets behind the workings of these theme parks—to everyone involved it is a real place, a real land, where all of these cartoon stories delight and come to life.

There may be characters in costumes, there might be hydraulic trickery in rides, there may be hidden roads and tunnels for behind-the-scenes-magic, yet for all intents and purposes, Disney never breaks form with the camera: you.

The blending of fact and fiction this requires in execution is no mean feat, especially in something as large and complex as a Disneyland, but this is exactly the feat that Disney out to do—and did, successfully.

By never deviating from the storyline of the Magic Kingdom, Disney has won converts in the millions while turning an enviable profit range and record, unparalleled in theme parks. Even calling Disneyland a theme park (which it is) seems paltry compared to the promise exuded by the sparkle and reputation the Magic Kingdom, relative to imitators, or 'competition'.

The truth is that Disney's belief in its story has made its theme parks and its movie empire (to name but two aspects) virtually unassailable to competition.

Discussion Questions:

What is your story?

_____

_____

_____

What is your story?

_____

_____

What is your story?

_____

_____

What is your story?

_____

_____

_____

What is your story?

_____

What is your story?

_____

What is your story?

_____

Secret 6. The stories are just fairy tales ("True Lies")

The fact that the stories may be a fiction you choose to believe in is underscored by the reality that in fact all successful brand archetypes are based on fairy tales! We call these 'true lies' after the 1994 Schwarzenegger film of the same title. Like Schwarzenegger's real character in the movie, the fairy tale is disguised under a more pedestrian cover.

From clear choices like Cinderella or Beauty and the Beast, film has long brought fairy tales to life on the big screen. But have you thought of other movies, from Pretty Woman to the Devil Wears Prada as also based on fairy tales? They are: it is just our fairy tale frequently wears a contemporary exterior shell and costumes.

Why is this? Fairy tales are repeated throughout the *gestalt* of our culture because the ideals they represent are on-going organizations of thought-wisdom that is transported this way. This is how every fairy tale is a 'true lie', that is, the details may lie, but what is underneath is not fantasy but rather, a basic truth.

There is a neatness to fairy tales that appeals on a deep psychological level. Beyond the obvious derring-do in many fairy tales of knights on horseback rescuing damsels in distress, there are subtler plot points that speak to heroism, to reason, to belief in oneself, in the power of love, and of loyalty.

There is a reason we talk of 'the moral of the story' for fairy tales are immensely entertaining lessons in being and becoming a better human being.

What stories and moods are evoked by the illustrations? How would you describe them to a blind person?

Discussion Questions:

What is your favourite fairy tale?

_____

Has it been made into a movie, a book, a game?

_____

_____

What popular movie, story, book or product embodies your fairy tale?

_____

_____

Are there competitive products that use the same story?

_____

How or why are competitors the same / different?

_____

_____

How can I see a fairy tale in a brand's story (unless it is Disney)?

_____

_____

_____

Does every story come down to a fairy tale?

_____

_____

Secret 7. There are only seven stories

There are only seven stories!? You have got to be kidding me, mister. There are dozens of stores. True that, however, with respect to a book on professional branding there are only seven stories.

Why is that? You will see that each of the seven stories gains significance when viewed from a certain perspective. You may also see that these points-of-view are logical outcomes from being human and therefore the number of them is constant.

I know there are far more than seven stories in life. In this book though, we are examining what we know works in brands and specifically what stories are exhibited by successful brands.

The fact that there is an infinite number of story variations is quite beside the point: the total number of fundamental stories exhibited by successful brands is just seven. This means that all successful brands fundamentally employ just one of seven archetypal behaviors in their design.

Does this mean that brand progenitors say at Coke or Pepsi sat down one day and said, 'hmm, I wonder which one of these types of behaviors we will model our brand on? Let's use number three!' No, but what it does mean is that through circumstance, luck or wit every one of the globe's top brands has hit on a successful formula, and uses it pretty much to the exclusion of all other strategies (until, or unless, they fail).

Understand there are hundreds of thousands of brands attempted in startup every year and very, very few ever succeed to the level of regional let alone national or global significance. The ones which do, do so for reasons that might be directly traced to their use (whether unwitting or deliberate) of the seven stories contained in the following section.

As you will see, even with just seven stories in use, there is plenty of room for variety: having a set of guidelines in fact streamlines and improve development of brand criteria, providing for finer overall detailing and more specific offers, copy and product development.

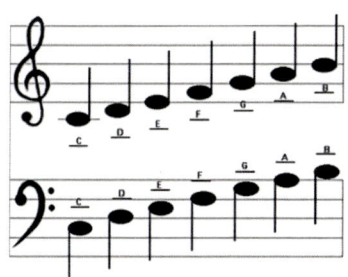

The essential quality, however, is to grasp your brand 'note' and become resonant with that note throughout your brand.

CROMA

Chromatic Residual Optimized Marketing Architectonics

D4
MarkBrand
CREATIVE

Color is the first and foremost emotional communicator of brand messaging.

D4 MarkBrand Creative has developed Chromatic Residual Optimized Marketing Architectonics (CROMA), a system which aids in the detailed specification of message-harmonic color ways for brands, branded environments and branded products.

Architectonics helps us understand which archetypal metaphors relate most closely to what colors.

CROMA separates branding messages into colored arrays.

1

VALIDATION SUCCESS

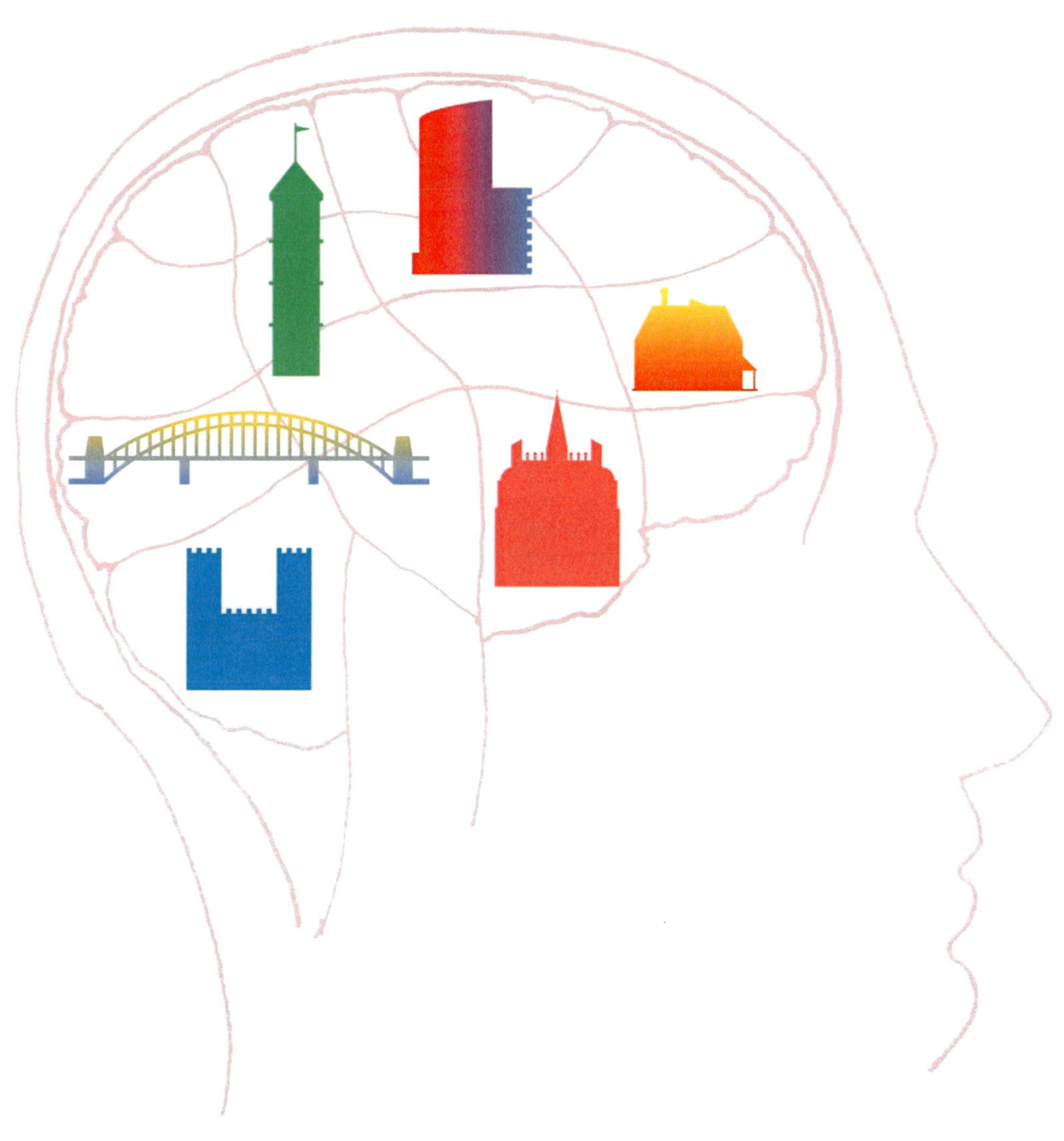

The Matriarchy
of Brands

The Matriarchy of Brands, while first documented here, are not an invention but more of a natural discovery. Like anything human that is real it is full of paradoxes but if you simply dive right in and get the gist of the matter, I am confident you may catch at least a glimpse of an entirely new access point to branding power.

We talk about a matriarchy of brands for a number of reasons.

1. First of all, we'd like to get clear that each type or sort of brand exists in relation to all others—which implies a social organization caste or structure.
2. Secondly, it bears repeating that most influential decision-makers of the discretionary economy are women, that is persons of the female gender, principally. Therefore, branding messages should as a general rule be constructed to be effective with a female audience.
3. The emphasis of the brand types may tip towards female gendered brand types even though there is an equal number of male types as female gendered brands, ever popular, have been on the upswing.

The Matriarchy of Brands is organized to display the entire family, from youngest to eldest and then all, together. The first two archetypes in our Matriarchy pertain to daughters, or brands of the female gender: House and Tower. The next two pertain to sons, or brands of the male gender: Bridge and Hotel. Next are 'parents', male Castle and female Palace. Finally, is the ensemble cast, the brand archetype of the family: Theatre.

Summing up, we have three female kinds of brands: House, Tower and Palace plus three male kinds of brands: Bridge, Hotel and Castle, and last, Theatre.

Within each of the brands types represented in the Matriarchy of Brands there are numerous successful examples illustrating nicely our key distinctions, which gives at once science plus example—often illustrating both what works—and what has not.

The distinctions suggested by having a what-has-been-until-now-hidden Matriarchy of Brands includes several pivotal ideas:

- Your competition is more about the brand type, that is to say, *emotion;* than the industry, niche or category or service;
- Meaning the emotional satisfaction is more important than the fact(s);
- The *relationship* is the key to brand happiness: *loyalty* is your trade;
- There is not nearly as much 'bandwidth' available as previously thought—one interpretation is that people have only about seven loyalty spots available and this crowds out redundancy;
- While getting clear on client or customer preferences is important it is vital to get clear about brand preferences and needs/requirements, as there is clearly no room for ambiguity with only seven formulae.

Looking through and absorbing this list makes clear why some details of the current economic landscape do not make logical sense, until we understand the different color lenses of "brand glasses" provided by the Matriarchy.

Correctly viewed, this spells opportunity. Brands communicate on a set of subtle emotional registers that appeal to certain types and kinds of people at certain times. They tend to be organized by business categories, like how we search for things on Google, but in reality, people tend to select based on emotional arrays, like how we judge successful dates.

Here, in a natural order for learning, are the seven members of the Matriarchy of Brands.

1. House
2. Tower
3. Bridge
4. Hotel
5. Castle
6. Palace
7. Theater

Archetype I: The House Brand

The At-Home Brand

Denny's, Phoenix Arizona, USA

The reliably down-home experience of the House Brand has perennial appeal. Even without the 'more-for-less' experience you get, there's an easy-going, homey quality to house brands that acts like a lowest common denominator in our society, allowing us to all have something we can agree about.

House Brand At-A-Glance Notes:

U Can't Touch This, MC Hammer

- The House Brand is a female archetype.
- Fundamental dweller within the archetype: Eldest daughter, the professional, in today's terms 'the working woman' ie. everyman
- Archetypal character: the Whore, in today's terms the "working woman" has become everywoman.
- Popular. Global examples: McDonald's, any do-it-yourself activity.
- Primary analysis: The House Brand presents anything everyday for sale at a predictable price. The value proposition of the House Brand is 'more for less' i.e. you'll get more 'stuff' for less 'loose change'.
- Color palettes: Red and Yellow/Gold.
- Popular American example: McDonald's (Red & Yellow).

Literally, the entry point of all branding, the House Brand is one of the most vital of all brand types in the marketplace. Without the House Brand there would be no yardstick to measure against, for House Brands are the 'all-brands' of branding. All the things that we think of *as* brands—consistent, reliable, easy and accessible—these are exactly what House Brands are about.

Yellow Taxis, above, of New York City are emblematic of House Brands and House Branding.

House brands are the workhorses of the brand economy. They rely on volume sales and mass appeal to create their special place in the market. It is anathema to a House Brand to appeal to specialized tastes or narrow needs, for the House Brand seeks out the requirements of the common man or woman and woos with the irresistible value and comfort of a home-cooked meal. Not for the House Brand are out-size budgets or gourmet tastes. House Brands don't cater to eccentric needs or out-of-control egos. No, the House Brand appeals to the practical, the down-to-earth, the easy-going, the comfortable and the frugal.

The house brand introduces a standard, or staple of branding: secret sauce, the *je ne sais quois** element. *French: literally "I do not know what".

In McDonald's terms, this is the Big Mac's "special sauce".

Product. The **Big Mac** consists of two 1.6 oz (45.4 g) beef patties, "special sauce" (a variant of Thousand Island dressing), iceberg lettuce, American cheese, pickles, and onions, served in a three-part sesame seed bun.

Big Mac - Wikipedia
https://en.wikipedia.org/wiki/Big_Mac

The Big Mac is branding's holy grail, ordinary grub dressed up through language of standards and repetition to represent an experience so predictable to a price-point that it is all but in-excludable. You *have* to experience a Big Mac. You *must* know what it is like. The special sauce *beckons*.

Some of the most profitable (and promiscuous) brands are House Brands. Creating sauce, er, success through the House Brand formula is not easy, for to be successful it must develop and master a delivery platform superior in efficiency to all competitors. Once successful, however, a well-positioned House Brand is very difficult to overturn, and it therefore grows and grows. Billions may be served.

House Brands are one of the most common, popular and interesting of all brand archetypes. Literally the foundation of branding, a House Brand is the first step beyond a purely generic or commodity product. Most people will be familiar with the concept of store brands, such as Safeway soup, or Rexall shampoo. These are House Brands. Retailers themselves can be house brands. Examples include McDonald's, Denny's and some supermarket store brands.

What is the purpose of a house brand? A house brand is there to provide inexpensively priced 'branded' experiences, that is to say consistent emotional quality and product deliverables at a lower price point than 'nationally advertised' brands. Never mind that our house brands are themselves nationally advertised! When you see price point packaging and everyday offers that are below mid-range alternatives you are likely experiencing a House Brand.

House Brands offer an acceptable alternative to higher priced forms of delivery for the masses. Most of us have purchased House Brand alternatives at one time or another—whether it is dishwashing detergent, paper towels or a hamburger, for convenience and economy's sake, the

House Brand frequently excels at introducing individuals to the brand economy.

As the most common archetype (who lives in a Palace nowadays?), the House Brand is instantly accessible to the widest number of consumers for everyday purchases. And, sometimes, the quality may be acceptable for on-going use. Some recent taste tastes have confirmed that McDonald's 88c coffee is as good as Starbucks (considerably more expensive cups!). Maybe this is because McDonald's is purportedly using Starbucks beans. Or maybe, McDonald's is simply committed to delivery on its unstated, House Brand promise.

House Brand Meta Communication:

The following eight variables in the Meta Communication of the House Brand are intended to stimulate further discussion, as well as to provide key inputs to the harmonic construct of the AMMM. For the terms in the last column, find brand specific substitutes for the brand you are studying and/or developing including detailed color codes and specific language or words plus statements.

Example brands are suggested.

HOUSE

I	Hue	Conscious	Color	Red + Yellow
II	Shape	Failsafe	Form	PREGNANT
III	Brand	Curious	Question	What do you want?
IIII	Elevator	Alternative	Answer	What you need.
V	Persona	Archetypal	Archetype	Whore 'working woman'
VI	Truth	Successful	Scent	Salty
VII	Secret	Perfect	Promise	More For Less
VIII	Architecture	Trustworthy	Texture	House
	FAILED: HUDSON'S BAY CO., BRATZ		SUPERMARKET BRANDS	DENNY'S
	POPULAR OLD SCHOOL			MCDONALD'S
	POPULAR NEW SCHOOL			LYFT
				WORDPRESS

Chapter Questions:

At what price level or point does a House Brand compete in the marketplace?

_____

Has it been made into a movie, a book, a game?

_____

What popular movie, story, book or product embodies this fairy tale?

_____

_____

What products, if any, in your category, use this story?

_____

_____

How or why are competitors the same / different?

_____

_____

What Disney characters inhabit the role of the 'working woman' character?

_____

What unique takes can you add, that do not contradict the story?

_____

_____

_____

_____

Archetype II: The Tower Brand

The 'Popular' Brand

Starbucks, Pike's Market, Seattle, USA

There is a unique quality to Tower Brands that make them irreplaceable in the eyes of their converts, belying their simple promise of popularity, related to feminine youth and beauty. The ultimate arbiter is social acceptance, which the Tower Brand takes on as its challenge, with aplomb.

Tower Brand-At-A-Glance Notes:

Stayin' Alive, Bee Gees

- Primary analysis: The Tower Brand creates its own universe where the primary attraction is the delivery of a sense of popularity and exclusivity to its converts.
- The Tower Brand is a feminine archetype.
- Color palettes: Generally, Kelly or Mid-Green with Black, OR Barbie Pink.
- Color analysis: The color refers to a youthful version of the feminine type where the potential for maturity is indicated but there is also a deep quality of transition or growth in process.
- Fundamental dweller within the archetype: Youngest daughter (the virgin)
- Popular Global examples: Starbucks (Green & Black), Barbie (Barbie Pink), The Body Shop

Kim Kardashian is a personification of Tower Branding; she says when your makeup is done, you just feel good. No surprise, in a candid moment, to see her carrying the proletarian symbol of popularity in hand, below.

Like the Bridge Brand, the Tower Brand occupies a mid-priced level in the branding world and is utilized by successful retailers and retail brands who are interested in promoting a lifestyle quality to their service experience and sell based on the quality of this experience more than on the basis of price.

Tower Brands can produce major sales volumes but do not compete on price, therefore their popularity is always limited to the number within the population who can afford their experience. It is no wonder then, that some of the most well-known and popular Tower Brands sell what are normally low-priced, even everyday items, but at a significant premium. Many people can afford a small splurge, and a Tower Brand is well positioned for this experience.

Ultimately, the Tower Brand connotes a strong sense of youth with a debutante's sense of sophisticated popularity. One key to maintaining profits for the Tower Brand is continual aesthetic innovation combined with a strong sense of identity and core values that remain stable. There is a strong undercurrent of sex appeal to the successful Tower Brand, but it is never overt. Rather, it is the covert 'forbidden' sex appeal of the adolescent virgin that rides just under the radar of the successful Tower Brand making it perennially appealing due to its clean-cut, fresh and always stylish nature.

Special Note regarding the color green and branding. Use the color green to associate your group, business or client with the environment at your peril.

While many groups, entrepreneurs and unknowing professionals have adopted Green as their color it is NOT the archetypal color for environmental causes. (This color is blue). Disregard this truism at your own risk.

Tower Brands demonstrate how people frequently confuse conscious (transitory) and unconscious (archetypal) association with colors. If there is also an environmental message it is absolutely secondary—the primary message of green is of youthful beauty, and therefore, of popularity and social acceptance.

The truth is brands get popular by being popular (ya, circular logic). However, for GREEN BRANDS, which ultimately make an unstated promise of popularity, it's actually a little easier. See, they actually have this cute little shortcut. All a GREEN BRAND has to do is *make its customers feel popular*. That's it! Once it succeeds at that, IT becomes popular. The rest, as they say, is history…

The Social Proof is in the Social Pudding

Thinking GREEN? Here are a few shortcuts to consider making your customers feel popular—and making your GREEN BRAND SUPER SUCCESSFUL:

1. Create an 'in the know' club-like atmosphere
2. Using special language and unique product identifiers is all part of the game (Tall non-fat frappocino anyone?)
3. Package using KELLY green exclusively (white or black as accents only)
4. Use female forms and shapes for logo design (think circular, tubular, curvilinear)
5. Make them wait (but not too, too long) for service (old night club trick)
6. Pack 'em in. Crowding people a little beyond their ordinary 'comfort zone' actually increases a sense of 'crowd security' if everyone in the crowd is 'part of the club'.

You don't need to throw away your GREEN BRAND idea—you DO need to 'frame it' or put it in a context of one of these universal human desires. Surprise: for 'green' brands, (that is, brands which communicate using the language and color of GREEN), this desire is unconsciously set around all things to do with social standing.

Being part of something popular—something bigger than oneself—and ultimately being personally popular within this context is the 'unstated promise' of every green brand!

Tower Brand Meta Communication:

The following eight variables in the Meta Communication of the Tower Brand are intended to stimulate further discussion, as well as to provide key inputs to the harmonic construct of the AMMM. For the terms in the last column, find brand specific substitutes for the brand you are studying and/or developing including detailed color codes and specific language or words plus statements.

Example brands are suggested.

TOWER

I	Hue	Conscious	Color	Green
II	Shape	Failsafe	Form	VIRGINAL
III	Brand	Curious	Question	Who do you think you are?
IIII	Elevator	Alternative	Answer	Popular
V	Persona	Archetypal	Archetype	Princess, locked in tower
VI	Truth	Successful	Scent	Baked
VII	Secret	Perfect	Promise	You, only better
VIII	Architecture	Trustworthy	Texture	Tower

FAILED: EDSEL		WHOLE FOODS	BARBIE, BODYSHOP
POPULAR OLD SCHOOL			STARBUCKS
POPULAR NEW SCHOOL			UBER

Chapter Questions:

At what price level or point does a Tower Brand compete in the marketplace?

_____

Has it been made into a movie, a book, a game?

_____

What popular movie, story, book or product embodies this fairy tale?

_____

What products, if any, in your category, use this story?

_____

_____

_____

How or why are competitors the same / different?

_____

_____

What Disney characters inhabit the role of the 'virgin' character?

_____

What unique takes can you add, that do not contradict the story?

_____

_____

_____

_____

Archetype III: The Bridge Brand

The 'Checkered Flag' Brand

1963 Chevrolet Corvette

The adventurous spirit of Bridge Brands breeds a feel of expansionism. Picture everyone experiencing the best aspects of a trip to Ikea, a Bridge Brand. Like Calvin Klein, these brands bring us up a notch quickly, having fun with us on the way. It's a guided trip, with a youthful spirit of fun and adventure.

Bridge Brand At-A-Glance Notes:

Can't Stop The Feeling, Justin Timberlake

- The Bridge Brand is a masculine archetype.
- Archetypal character: the knight, or in modern terms—the jock
- Popular Global examples: BMW, Harley-Davidson, Ikea.
- Primary analysis: The Bridge Brand presents its own mid-priced universe where the primary attraction is a combination of community and experience notable for its sense of adventure.
- Color palettes: Generally, Gold with Black, Navy or sometimes Purple, it may also be represented by Yellow/Gold and Navy.
- Color analysis: The color combinations refer to a youthful version of the masculine type where maturity is indicated but there is also a quality of transition or growth in process.
- Not to be confused with: The House Brand, even with Wal-Mart, is not first about the price, it is experience. The promise is different.

First past the checkered flag: the image connotes auto racing, specifically, Formula One and top speed, performance records and industry racing records. To men especially, there is an innate appeal to performance for performance's sake. Brands like BMW, Harley-Davidson, and even, to a lesser but more commonly available start, so do Chevrolet, IKEA and Calvin Klein because each has a quality of transition and requisite energy, aka excitement that goes with a spirit of adventure.

The Bridge Brand appeals to the adventure part of our mind, where we seek change of moving past ordinary or mundane to higher reaches. This is the area of many brand wars, i.e. Chevrolet Corvette vs. Ford Mustang, for instance.

Anyone in fashion probably recognizes the 'bridge brand' to represent those labels which, magically, sometimes 'bridge' the experience between very high fashion with everyday wear. Brands like Polo, Ralph Lauren, Calvin Klein and hundreds of others regularly produce bridge brand products that command a higher price point than house brands in return for a. superior experience.

This area represents an extremely wide swath of opportunity as the promise of the Bridge Brand is fundamentally about quality—a range of qualities, to be precise, that always stretches from one continuum to another. For instance, from machine-made to hand-stitched. The Bridge Brand may present an alternate, or substitute for the one-off product at an out-of-reach price point, with a superior machine-made product with hand detailing, at a middle price.

A survey of automotive brands, which have profited from this brand strategy is instructive for it encompasses an extremely wide range of cars, price points and decision-makers: Audi, BMW, Chevrolet, Harley-Davidson, and Peugeot.

The Bridge Brand is a powerful, fun archetype commonly employed in the fashion world, and also, subtly in the automotive world, as well. Bridge Brands offers significant and unique advantages in service delivery. The Bridge Brand, more than many other archetypes stands for a specific qualitative flavor of service delivery. There is an accessible nature to Bridge Brands that belies the notable quality of their service experience.

Bridge Brands are for many consumers their first foray into a 'brand experience' beyond the House Brand. Typically, Bridge Brands are priced as a 'bridge' between less expensive House Brands and more expensive name brands, such as the Castle or Palace archetypes. In the rush to specialize the intermediate territory of the Bridge Brand has been abandoned by many marketers; who perhaps see it as a mere 'stepping

stone' in the market middle. What may be missing is a clear understanding of the true characteristic of the Bridge Brand, which is neither a cheaper version of name brand, nor a pricier version of house brand, but rather its own unique quirks of fun as well as adventure in a safe, sanitized environment.

Some of the most interesting (and profitable) consumer brands are Bridge Brands. Successful Bridge Brands inevitably have a distinct, even quirky quality that makes them extremely memorable. They have a youthful quality combined with a degree of maturity that makes them palatable, and even attractive to a variety of age groups. There is a sense in the successful Bridge Brand that it makes up its own universe—one where it is the center and the salvation. This can create powerful loyalties and extremely strong lifetime brand relationships. The successfully conceived Bridge Brand is certainly much more than just a stepping-stone—it is a destination experience.

If you are prepared to guide your customer by holding them by the hand, metaphorically at least, then you may be thinking of a Bridge Brand. The successful Bridge Brand sweeps in on horseback, rescues the 'damsel in distress' from the chaos around her, then rushes her across the bridge to a place of security, before safely depositing her in a new, elevated situation.

Think of the relationship of the knight on horseback with the damsel in distress as comparable to that of your brand with your clientele. If there is no aspect of this in your relationship, then this brand metaphor is not for you or this brand. If it is, then look to see what other aspects may be present as well.

Bridge brands fulfill a vital and profitable spectrum of the brand economy. Despite this, they remain an underutilized and one of the least-exploited successfully demonstrated forms of branding.

There's no reason for this. Ikea, Harley-Davidson and Visa are three quite different brands, which nevertheless all utilize this same formula, borrowed from the fashion industry. The promise of getting 'more than you paid for' is what they all deliver on.

That they do so in a way which often surprises and delights is just part of their charm.

In the rush to specialize, the intermediate territory of the Bridge Brand has been abandoned by many marketers; who perhaps see it as a mere 'stepping stone' in the market middle. What may be missing is a clear understanding of the true characteristic of the Bridge Brand, which is neither a cheaper version of name brand, nor a pricier version of house brand, but rather its own unique quality of fun and adventure at an approachable price-point.

Successful Bridge brands such as Harley Davidson or Marlboro are successes in large part simply because by the act of co-branding they are conforming to their natural type. Both Harley and Marlboro are archetypal Bridge brands that use this to their advantage over a wide range of products beyond the original anchor. Bridge brands are inhabited by Knights. The Bridge brand offers a masculine 'escape from reality' quality that works well with a variety of products and translate well so long as they answer the question "how?".

Some of the most interesting (and profitable) consumer brands are Bridge Brands. Successful Bridge Brands have a distinct, even quirky quality that makes them extremely memorable. They have a youthful quality combined with a degree of maturity that makes them palatable, and even attractive to a variety of age groups. There is a sense in the successful Bridge Brand that it makes up its own universe—one where it is the center and the salvation. This can create powerful loyalties and extremely strong lifetime brand relationships. The successfully conceived Bridge Brand is certainly much more than just a stepping-stone—it is a destination experience.

When to use it:

Use the Bridge Brand format when you're prepared to stand out in a crowded marketplace, (BlackBerry!). This marque requires confidence and the backing of solid products. For many consumers it will be their first foray into a 'brand experience' beyond the House Brand. Typically, Bridge Brands are priced as a 'bridge' between less expensive House Brands and more expensive 'designer' brands, such as the Castle or Palace archetypes. However, there are no hard rules about price or position. If your category (niche) is overcrowded, for instance with Castle or Palace brands, choosing the Bridge formula can be a recipe to succeed with a distinct offer. Your brand will become a connecting point to others–strategically an excellent place to be!

Bridge Brand Meta Communication:

The following eight variables in the Meta Communication of the Bridge Brand are intended to stimulate further discussion, as well as to provide key inputs to the harmonic construct of the AMMM. For the terms in the last column, find brand specific substitutes for the brand you are studying and/or developing including detailed color codes and specific language or words plus statements.

Example brands are suggested.

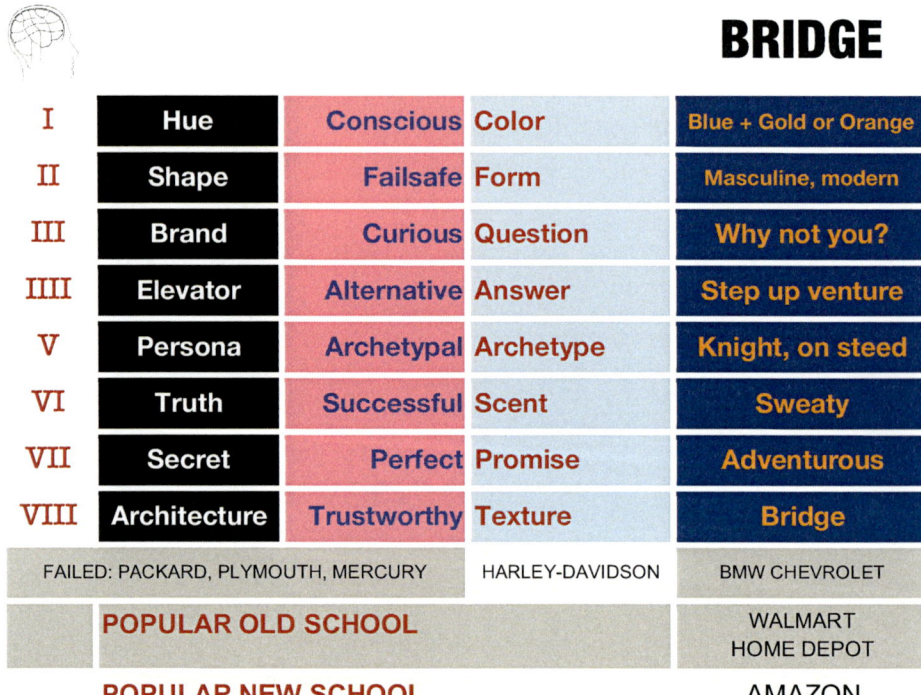

BRIDGE

I	Hue	Conscious	Color	Blue + Gold or Orange
II	Shape	Failsafe	Form	Masculine, modern
III	Brand	Curious	Question	Why not you?
IIII	Elevator	Alternative	Answer	Step up venture
V	Persona	Archetypal	Archetype	Knight, on steed
VI	Truth	Successful	Scent	Sweaty
VII	Secret	Perfect	Promise	Adventurous
VIII	Architecture	Trustworthy	Texture	Bridge
	FAILED: PACKARD, PLYMOUTH, MERCURY		HARLEY-DAVIDSON	BMW CHEVROLET
	POPULAR OLD SCHOOL			WALMART HOME DEPOT
	POPULAR NEW SCHOOL			AMAZON

Chapter Questions:

At what price level or point does a Bridge Brand compete in the marketplace?

_____

Has it been made into a movie, a book, a game?

_____

What popular movie, story, book or product embodies this fairy tale?

_____

What products, if any, in your category, use this story?

_____

_____

How or why are competitors the same / different?

_____

What Disney characters inhabit the role of the 'knight' character?

_____

_____

_____

What unique takes can you add, that do not contradict the story?

_____

_____

_____

_____

Archetype IIII: The Hotel Brand

The 'Choice' Brand

The Gulf Hotel Bahrain

Picture a grand hotel! Inside its elaborate and gilded sliding doors is a large and welcoming lobby. Plushly carpeted and serviced with numerous uniformed attendants. On one side is a long check-in desk. On another is a Concierge desk, staffed by a very knowledgeable person willing to help you with almost anything. Further on, there are boutiques, including a sweet shop, coffee shop, gift store and shoe shine. Up the stairs is a fine dining room, while tucked away to one side is a bar. Which way to go?

Hotel Brand At-A-Glance Notes:

Uptown Funk, Mark Ronson

- Primary analysis: The Hotel Brand trades on a promise of choice and chance. Ultimately those loyal to Hotel Brands are purchasing an experience of transformation.
- The Hotel Brand is a masculine archetype with a feminine frame.
- Color palettes: Red, White and Blue.
- Color analysis: The Red refers to the feminine type while the Blue refers to the masculine. The White refers to the gap between them and also the bridge of transformation.
- Fundamental dweller within the archetype: Youngest son (the flame)
- Popular Global examples: Pepsi and Danone.

Here is a boutique brand. As the fourth archetype, the boutique concept connects at one extreme as the destination for the adventurous character of a Bridge, while on another level they connect with the security of a Castle.

What does this mean as far as focus and drive? Hotels profit through focus and concentration on a core customer. Paradoxically, since the Hotel Brand delivers on a promise of transformation, the successful Hotel is all about consistency. This makes sense when you realize the ideal background for change (growth) is consistency. Hotels are all about choice, discovery and change! The ideal hotel experience leaves you refreshed, invigorated and ready to take on the world.

The hotel brand is a distinct and revolutionary brand type that delivers transformation, through consistency of experience. Hotel brands are particularly popular in America, where both Pepsi and Tommy Hilfiger hail from. Both of these popular brands compete head to head with other popular brands of differing types. Pepsi with Coke; Tommy with Ralph. Yet, due to their distinct promise and unique flavor they are able to compete and hold their own even with much older, well-established competition. Pepsi, unlike Coke, is the "choice of a New Generation". This allows it to compete head to head with a virtually identical product, in almost identical packaging at an identical price point (and side by side on the same grocery store shelf).

The Hotel Brand is a unique blend of energies offering a distinct promise of transformation that can exist at many price and service levels. The promise of the outcome is equal to the experience itself for the Hotel Brand.

Hotel Brands have a service quality that tends to provide a wide band of market service. The challenge for all brands is staying focused on core customers. For Hotel Brands, which aim to please through an experience that transforms, this can be an extra challenge. With such a wide promise, Hotel brands must deliver qualitative convenience, and typically do so with either a wide variety of choices, many locations, or both.

The successful Hotel Brand excels at both innovation and widespread service delivery. In doing so, it may compete profitably against more narrowly focused brands indefinitely, in market segments that afford sufficient on-going advertising to promote their message of change. Hotel Brands must plan strategically for the fact that while the brand is ultimately providing change, change of loyalty is anathema to brands and branding. Therefore, there is a fine line to be held. One thing going for Hotel Brands is that America, Australia, Britain and France all conform to the Hotel Brand as national archetypes, therefore the fundamental message and color scheme of the Hotel Brand naturally resonates in these communities.

Hotel Brand Strategy relies on the formula:

CHOICE => CHANCE => CHANGE => TRANSFORMATION

All Hotel Brands thrive by providing a choice of options through which an experience of chance is provided that creates a change of state. The change provides for the opportunity to product transformation: one of the greatest brand rewards. Although we do not necessarily subscribe to Maslow's hierarchy directly in terms of the Matriarchy of Brands, you can see below

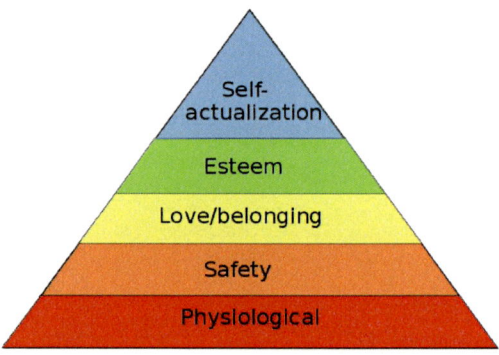

that the Hotel Brand promise is on the higher levels of life's needs.

Hotel Brands naturally aspire to deliver some of the higher levels, indicated by Maslow's hierarchy of needs, represented as a pyramid, above. Pepsi's frequently evolving logo-type is typical of Hotel Branding, as expressed in design.

Four Fundamental Ways of Relating

Four fundamental human perspectives have been identified. All brand types must form their own strategy: Each type may be predicted to relate with the 'Concierge' characteristics of the Hotel Brand in a specific way.

Perspective	To The World	Method of Relating	Unspoken Inquiry to Hotel Brand
Architect	Powerful	Planning from Past Time Experience	**Which Way… should I connect my strategy with yours?**
Engineer	Empathic	Experience All Time Moment Relationships	**Who can I connect with here?**
Designer	Active	Present Time Actions	**Which way do I care to play / what are my choices?**
Builder	Key	Future Time Results	**What can I do next?**

You will have a strategy in place to deal with each of the four perspectives because 80–90% of people can be identified with one of these perspectives almost immediately. Knowing what you will say to them when you meet them is merely good planning! Remember that your brand will meet people in all kinds of ways, include:

- In-person, through physical presence.
- In-person, through somebody you know.
- Over the Internet through your home page.
- Over the Internet through another page / landing page.
- Over the Internet through Social Media, i.e. YouTube or Facebook.
- Through your book or other printed story medium.
- At an event.
- What else?

The following eight variables in the Meta Communication of the Bridge Brand are intended to stimulate further discussion, as well as to provide key inputs to the harmonic construct of the AMMM. For the terms in the last column, find brand specific substitutes for the brand you are studying and/or developing including detailed color codes and specific language or words plus statements.

Example brands are suggested.

HOTEL

I	Hue	Conscious	Color	Contrast Pair
II	Shape	Failsafe	Form	H BARBELL TRACK
III	Brand	Curious	Question	Which way R U going?
IIII	Elevator	Alternative	Answer	Choice
V	Persona	Archetypal	Archetype	Concierge
VI	Truth	Successful	Scent	Transformation
VII	Secret	Perfect	Promise	Too cool for school
VIII	Architecture	Trustworthy	Texture	Hotel
	FAILED: AMC, STUDEBAKER			GM
	POPULAR OLD SCHOOL			PEPSICO
	POPULAR NEW SCHOOL			TWITTER
				AIRBNB

Chapter Questions:

At what price level or point does a Hotel Brand compete in the marketplace?

_____

Has it been made into a movie, a book, a game?

_____

What popular movie, story, book or product embodies this story?

_____

What products, if any, in your category, use this story?

_____

How or why are competitors the same / different?

_____

What Disney characters inhabit the role of the 'concierge' character?

_____

What strategies can be developed that position with this brand comfortably, profitably and simultaneously with all these inquiries? What is the path of least resistance? What is the path of greatest profit margin? What path employs all the skills and experience on your team to greatest effect?

_____

_____

_____

_____

Archetype V: The Castle Brand

The 'Safety' Brand

Bodiam Castle, East Susses, UK

There is a utility-like quality to Castle Brands: even while frequently addressing luxury needs, Castle brands, like Mercedes-Benz exhibit a functional, purposeful quality that traditionally errs on the conservative side. No wonder that utilities frequently gravitate to this archetype naturally.

Castle Brand At-A-Glance Notes:

Don't You Worry 'bout a thing, Stevie Wonder, etc...
Don't Worry Be Happy, Pharrell Williams

- Primary analysis: The Castle Brand trades on a promise of safety. Fundamentally Castle Brands promise security or 'everywhere'.
- The Castle Brand is a masculine archetype.
- Color palettes: Blue (and White) OR Black (and White).
- Color analysis: The Blue refers to the masculine type—specifically to the sky, home of the creator, while the White refers to the possibility surrounding it.
- Fundamental dweller within the archetype: Father (the king)
- Popular Global examples: Adidas, Ford, IBM, Facebook, LinkedIn, Mercedes-Benz; retailer example: GAP stores

Countering and contrasting the female anchor of the Palace Brand, Castle brands are the male version archetype in the matriarchy of brands. Like a Palace brand, the Castle brand works well on a stable platform of design, but its distinctly masculine qualities, query and answers have not only a very different flavor, but a differing premise as well.

The Castle Brand stands close to the top in terms of aspiration. Most importantly, however, it trades on its reputation for reliability and even more, safety, to develop its strong loyalties and perennial profits. The conservative nature of Castle Brands perfectly echoes the sensibilities of their clientele who are motivated more by consistency and concern for their own welfare than by price.

Castle Brands include some of the most stalwart brands in the world, though typically not those at the highest reaches of price, nor those below the median. The concern for quality is so important to Castle Brands that it is unlikely for them to serve below a certain price-point where they feel quality or distribution might suffer. Likewise, their need to be of service to many prevents them from climbing to the most rarified levels of price.

The solid and proven way is the way of the Castle Brand. While generally among the least glamorous of Brand types (utilities are typically Castle Brands), making them among the least suitable for fashion, their reputation for reliability makes them ideal for products or services with a repeating or steady nature.

Promotional aspects to develop with Castle Brands include the idea of multiple location or 'everywhere' offers, refer others offers, as well as direct season-related offers as requested by the industry your brand participates in. Other things being equal, Blue 'castle brands', like Ford, thrive best when they can strike out on their own with a bold new product and promise, like Ford's original Model T.

The Ford Model T did not require special promotional offers: in fact, Ford successively reduced the price from $825 in 1908 to under $300 in 1925, as the enormous scale of production reduced costs through mass efficiencies, while also increasing his employees' wages far above the norm of the day.

Castle Brand Meta Communication:

The following eight variables in the Meta Communication of the Castle Brand are intended to stimulate further discussion, as well as to provide key inputs to the harmonic construct of the AMMM. For the terms in the last column, find brand specific substitutes for the brand you are studying and/or developing including detailed color codes and specific language or words plus statements.

Example brands are suggested as is background mood.

CASTLE

I	Hue	Conscious	Color	Blue
II	Shape	Failsafe	Form	BLOCK-SHAPED
III	Brand	Curious	Question	Where are you going to?
IIII	Elevator	Alternative	Answer	Everywhere
V	Persona	Archetypal	Archetype	King
VI	Truth	Successful	Scent	Home
VII	Secret	Perfect	Promise	Security
VIII	Architecture	Trustworthy	Texture	Castle
	FAILED: TUCKER		MERCEDES-BENZ	FORD
	POPULAR OLD SCHOOL			IBM MICROSOFT
	POPULAR NEW SCHOOL			FACEBOOK
				TESLA

Chapter Questions:

At what price level or point does a Castle Brand compete in the marketplace?

_____

Has it been made into a movie, a book, a game?

_____

What popular movie, story, book or product embodies this story?

_____

What products, if any, in your category, use this story?

_____

_____

_____

How or why are competitors the same / different?

_____

What Disney characters inhabit the role of the 'King' character?

_____

What unique takes can you add, that do not contradict the story?

_____

_____

_____

_____

Archetype VI: The Palace Brand
The 'Always' Brand

Vintage Coca-Cola Advertisement.

While associated with things that have been around 'forever', frequently it is the other way around. Cultural symbols like Santa Claus, and the Spirit of Ecstasy are cultural icons created by resonant Palace Brands that have unequivocally eclipsed their origins, winning the game resonantly for such brands. These two brands demonstrate the power of effective brand strategies.

Palace Brand At-A-Glance Notes
I'd Like To Teach The World to Sing

- Primary analysis: The Palace Brand trades on a promise of timelessness. Fundamentally Palace Brands promise eternity or immortality.
- The Palace Brand is a feminine archetype.
- Color palettes: Red (and White—may also include silver or other faint accents) OR Black (and White).
- Color analysis: The Red refers to the feminine type—specifically to the blood of birth, while the White refers to the possibility surrounding it.
- Fundamental dweller within the archetype: Mother (the queen or empress)
- Popular Global examples: Apple, Chrysler, Coca-Cola, CHANEL, Fiat, Rolls-Royce and Toyota.

The *Spirit of Ecstasy* was designed in 1909. The design, by artist Charles Sykes is a figurine that, to this day, is an exclusive addition to every Rolls-Royce car.

Launched in 1909 the Spirit of Ecstasy is described today by Rolls-Royce as "challenging the social conventions of the time" to "encapsulate the pursuit of personal liberty, and freedom from conformity". In fact, her appearance did become iconic, as did Coca-Cola's finessing of Santa Claus. In both cases, such uses helped establish the brand quickly. Today, Rolls-Royce is an outsize brand with an outsize personality and outsize brand value—and prices. It is instructive that it has been in effective use of this strategy for over 100 years.

The Palace Brand is a powerful type that can work for timeless name brands at all price levels. The key is that while, like all brands, Palace Brands must at some level innovate, while at another level they must never change. The loyalty that customers have to Palace Brands is at the level of 'motherhood and apple pie' meaning that change is really very aggravating to their sensibilities and any change may be cause for revolt.

Palace Brands include some of the most popular brands in the world, as well as some of the most lofty and desired brands. Palace Brands maintain an aura of mystique combined with a material familiarity that is redolent of both home and hearth while also having a hint of something just beyond definition, or explanation. Most successful Palace Brands capitalize on initial excellent positioning and build long-term success by gradually building up an inventory of brand collateral cues that stimulate an invincible armory of emotionally redolent memories with their customers over time.

The ultimate promise of immortality behind the Palace Brand, is so obviously undeliverable, that ironically the Palace promise is one of the most believed and iron-clad of brand types. Palace Brands trade on product integrity and reputation more than any other brand type. When they break this promise, all havoc breaks loose, but again, they are so strong they normally adjust, make amends and pick up where they left off. Their customers always return once they return to their original promise.

Palace brands, like CHANEL require little, if any change to substance along the way. Most of all, they need confident creative people who understand the rules and then are willing to 'feel' the best way to implement them along the way, while breaking few, if any rules. Real

Palace brands, like CHANEL, Coca-Cola, Apple and Aveda broke the rules early.

Coco Chanel rewrote the rules of fashion for women, by cutting clothes shaped originally for men, for the female figure. She developed a way to cut fabric on the bias that create a simple jersey dress that fit like no other. And she created the fashion for big, chunky costumed jewelry that pervades to this day. What else does a fashion house that has innovated so many ways need in the way of gimmicks, risks and change? The answer, clearly, is nothing!

The Palace Brand is about timelessness. Coca-Cola knows this, now. So does Apple. So do Aveda and CHANEL. Interestingly, all of these companies are continuously introducing new products and campaigns, but the gestalt of all successful Palace Brands is remarkably implacable. No matter the latest fashion, trend or technology these giants of branding continue to succeed with remarkably simple esthetics, design and simple, timeless innovations that perennially reach a wide, receptive audience.

In a world that is constantly changing we need Palace Brands to remind us that it's not all about the latest trend. Even Apple, as the technology representative among this tribe, has remained remarkable unchanged (relative to other technology giants, like Microsoft or IBM) in philosophy, design and interface. Obviously, fashion companies and technology giants make their money through change, so how is they can simultaneously remain the same? This is what creates the epicenter of a Palace Brand—the unchangeable, central elements which may be tweaked and tuned, but never really altered. Notice too, that logos and graphic representation for all of these brands have been static for years. After all, perennial good taste never goes out of style. And for the *cognoscenti* (that's Palace Brand talk for fans) good taste is where it's at!

Determine the core design, visual and thematic elements. Innovate the heck out of them, then leave 'em alone. Make, thoughtful changes only.

Emphasize design in marketing and advertising. Style is something that comes and go, but good quality design always looks good. Emphasize material quality and finish in manufactured goods. Apple's computers are 'milled from a solid piece of aluminum', CHANEL's skirts are invisibly weighted at the back with a small chain on the inside to ensure the garment keeps its lines as you walk down the street. Coca-Cola early on insisted on a unique and timeless anthropomorphic bottle design. And so it goes...

The Palace Brand archetype is inhabited by the eternal Mother. What are her qualities? Mother always cares, always loves, is always there, no matter what. No wonder that Palace brands answer the unstated question "When?" with the unstated answer "Forever". It's 'always Coca-Cola'.

The Palace metaphor presents a timeless backdrop to brands, brand experiences, and user experiences. The fundamental domain of the Palace archetype is Time. Query the Palace (brand, UX, or design) and the default question is always the categorical 'When'? The only answer the Palace will give in response to this question is 'Forever', or 'Always'. In other words, the Palace archetype, exhibited by brands such as Apple, Coca-Cola and CHANEL (yes, the Coco Chanel's CHANEL) is the archetype of the eternal mother.

Since the unspoken promise returned by this archetype is both strong and unequivocal, it gives a pretty good sense of what should be coming. And, for the most part, at least in packaging/box design, Apple succeeds brilliantly. Apple hardware products are very timeless in appearance; do not really subscribe to fads, thus retaining an elegant, understated quality.

Unfortunately, in terms of the UX experience, especially in newer products like Apple's iOS mobile operating system, timeless is not what is experienced. Minimal? Yes. Forever? No. As a matter of fact, the experience of the entire user interface is one of continuous adaptive discovery. This represents a design archetype (of the Adventurer) that might be a great place to start for a game designer, but it does not make sense for Apple. Apple's UX experience should be solid, constant, clear, and consistent. Underlying architectural elements of the Palace ought to preemptively prevent any other type of design from emerging. Time will tell.

Apple's iconic Manhattan store, above. Putting Apple's Palace Brand chemistry into a seamlessly integrated product experience from top to bottom is an Herculean task that has proved to be a highly profitable strategy for Apple shareholders.

Palace Brand Meta Communication:

The following eight variables in the Meta Communication of the Palace Brand are intended to stimulate further discussion, as well as to provide key inputs to the harmonic construct of the AMMM. For the terms in the last column, find brand specific substitutes for the brand you are studying and/or developing including detailed color codes and specific language or words plus statements.

Example brands are suggested.

PALACE

I	Hue	Conscious	Color	Red
II	Shape	Failsafe	Form	Anthropomorphic
III	Brand	Curious	Question	When?
IIII	Elevator	Alternative	Answer	Permanence
V	Persona	Archetypal	Archetype	Queen
VI	Truth	Successful	Scent	Sweet
VII	Secret	Perfect	Promise	always, forever
VIII	Architecture	Trustworthy	Texture	Palace
	FAILED: SATURN		FIAT	CHRYSLER
	POPULAR OLD SCHOOL			COCA-COLA
	POPULAR NEW SCHOOL			APPLE
				NETFLIX

Chapter Questions:

At what price level or point does a Palace Brand compete in the marketplace?

_____

Has it been made into a movie, a book, a game?

_____

What popular movie, story, book or product embodies this story?

_____

What products, if any, in your category, use this story?

_____

_____

_____

_____

How or why are competitors the same / different?

_____

What Disney characters inhabit the role of the 'Queen' character?

_____

What unique takes can you add, that do not contradict the story?

_____

_____

_____

_____

Archetype VII: The Theater Brand

The 'Party' Brand

The Orpheum Theatre, Vancouver, Canada

The excitement of the red carpet in the preparation of a live theatrical performance is not dissimilar to the attention to detail the Honda puts into engineering. One of dozens of famous quotes of Soichiro Honda is "Raise the sail with your stronger hand", meaning that you must go after the opportunities in life that you are best equipped to do. The passion this implies, inviting as it does co-creation with others—that is theater branding.

Theater Brand At-A-Glance Notes:

Party Rock Anthem, LMFAO

- Primary analysis: The Theater Brand trades on a promise of unity. Basically, these brands are the 'how to' brands of humanity.
- The Theater Brand is gender neutral within a Matriarchy.
- Color palettes: Red and White alone, OR Polychrome (any/all colors may be used, especially rainbow-style, i.e. Google).
- Color analysis: The various colors of the Theater Brand refer to the distinctly different personalities united by the brand, each of which may co-exist without losing its uniqueness.
- Color analysis: The Red refers to the feminine type—specifically to the blood of birth, while the White refers to the possibility surrounding it.
- Fundamental dweller of the archetype: The Family / Theater Co.
- Popular Global examples: 3M, eBay, Google, Honda

Google

The theater brand is a relatively new brand type, which works well for companies that embrace new working paradigms. The concept comes from the example of a theater company where there are a variety of roles, which must be filled (writer, director, producer, stage designer, actors, and so on) and the prevailing modus is 'the show must go on'. Theater companies often have an intimate family-like atmosphere and a flat level of decision-making rather than the traditional hierarchy. This, coupled with the theatrical idea of improvisation makes theater brands ideal for the new economy.

Leading examples of theater brands include Google and 3M (maker of numerous innovative products like Post-its and Scotch brand tape, to name two of thousands). Google is notorious for its extraordinary working environment, which includes play areas, free food and dozens of other workplace innovations. At 3M one of the most famous stories is how one of the secretaries in the 70s {check data} came up with a use for the repositionable adhesive that no one else saw an application for. The Post-it note was born.

The Theater brand is a relatively new archetype in branding. It emerged recently for reasons that business structure, until recently was not receptive to its format. The Theater Brand is the 'how to' brand that delivers with a community response. Now that the Theater Brand has emerged its polychrome nature is really coming out of the closet and beginning to sparkle. Theater brands thrive on big challenges and big ideas. Because of this they are often uniquely organized business entities.

Some of the newest and fastest-rising brands (for instance internet properties) are Theater Brands. Many of the most innovative, useful and even ubiquitous products come from Theater Brand environments. Theater Brands deliver on promises that cannot be easily created in small spaces and they sustain their extraordinary levels of innovation through group participation and input.

Creating success with a Theater Brand requires a commitment to cooperative working arrangements and a pluralistic view of success. After all, a successful Theatre cannot thrive forever on one production alone, no matter how popular. This may be why successful Theater Brands create cultures that are driven to invent, innovate and even change the way the world works.

Theater Brand strategies have a 'the show must go on' spirit and quality to them. There is frequently a moving element, or other entertainment-inspired or spectacular ornamentation to the strategy, which intends to inspire and delight and involve, ultimately inciting action. They are great at turning out tons of products:

A few of the plethora of brands from just two Theater Brands, illustrated on this page.

How is Honda a Theater Brand? Soichiro Honda, who like Coco Chanel, has plugged personal DNA into the namesake brand; is quoted as saying, "If you hire only those people you understand, the company will never get people better than you are. Always remember that you often find outstanding people among those you don't particularly like. Honda works internally like a Theater company, and externally with a singular face, more or less like Disney, keeping it down to a couple external brands to handle a huge range of well-engineered products from lawn mowers to outboard engines, on up.

At right is a concept for a commemorative edition of the highest selling vehicle ever, the Honda Super Cub. This is for the **100 Millionth** Commemorative Edition!

Below, the Honda NSX hybrid sports car powered by 3.5 L twin-turbo V6 engine and three electric motors, with "SH-AWD" all-wheel drive, capable of close to 600 horsepower. The transmission is a 9-speed dual-clutch semi-automatic.

Theater brands use group dynamics successfully levering people of diverse talents and abilities to contribute their best in a "let's all put ourselves behind this idea" kind of way. It's how Roy and Walt Disney made Disney, as well.

Theater Brand Meta Communication:

The following eight variables in the Meta Communication of the Theater Brand are intended to stimulate further discussion, as well as to provide key inputs to the harmonic construct of the AMMM. For the terms in the last column, find brand specific substitutes for the brand you are studying and/or developing including detailed color codes and specific language or words plus statements. Example brands are suggested.

THEATER

I	Hue	Conscious	Color	Rainbow
II	Shape	Failsafe	Form	Anthropomorphic/ Corinthian
III	Brand	Curious	Question	How?
IIII	Elevator	Alternative	Answer	Inclusion
V	Persona	Archetypal	Archetype	Family
VI	Truth	Successful	Scent	Hot Butter
VII	Secret	Perfect	Promise	Together
VIII	Architecture	Trustworthy	Texture	Theater
	NOT LIVING UP TO IT: CADILLAC		3M	POST-IT NOTES SCOTCH TAPE
	POPULAR OLD SCHOOL			DISNEY
	POPULAR NEW SCHOOL			GOOGLE

Chapter Questions:

At what price level or point does a Theater Brand compete in the marketplace?

_____

Has it been made into a movie, a book, a game?

_____

What popular movie, story, book or product embodies this story?

_____

What products, if any, in your category, use this story?

_____

How or why are competitors the same / different?

_____

What Disney characters inhabit the role of the 'Family' character?

_____

_____

_____

What unique takes can you add, that do not contradict the story?

_____

_____

_____

_____

_____

MARKKO

Monetized Achievement Residual Key Knowledge Optimization

D4
MarkBrand
CREATIVE

Form, including words, sounds and marks, is the primary intellectual communicator of brand messaging.

D4 MarkBrand Creative has developed Monetized Achievement Residual Key Knowledge Optimization (MARKKO), a technique which allows the monetization of key aspects of a brand's knowledge-base.

Architectonics helps us understand which archetypal metaphors relate most closely to what sounds and forms.

MARKKO expresses branded messages into harmonic profit centers.

2

AUTHENTICATION SUCCESS

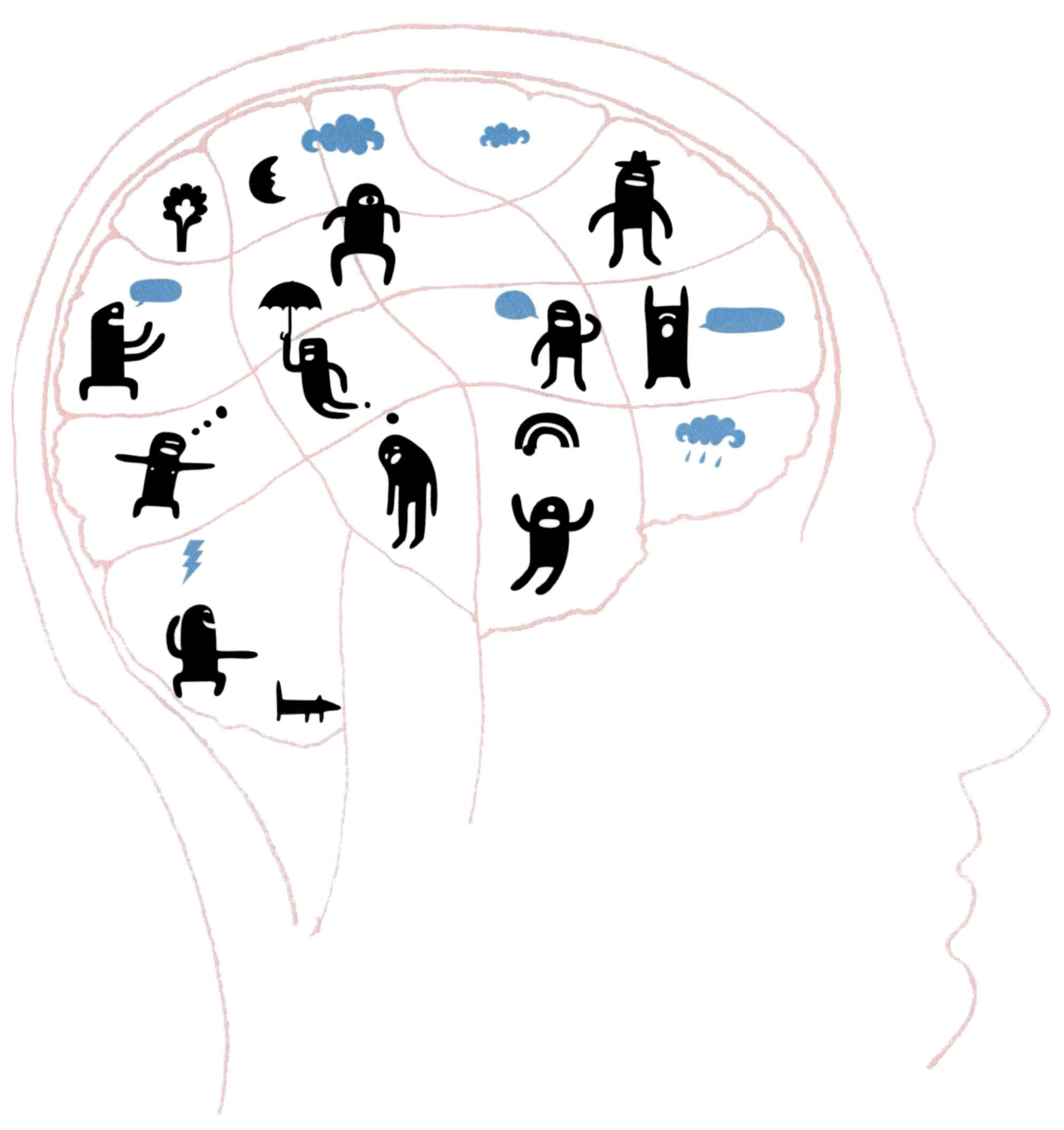

Branding for Profit

"Now what?" you may be thinking. How can I begin to learn how to do more business with this stuff?

Hold on cowboy! Have I not been guiding you all the way, already? Could I not hold the reins a few more miles before leaving you the driver's seat? First off, I'd like to know that you understand a couple of things:

- What I learned about branding from selling CIGARETTES
- Why Coke and Pepsi are rivals, NOT competitors
- How brands REALLY work in practice
- What is Brand Identification and
- What is Emotional Gap

It is my hope you will learn how to develop and use ever-more productive strategies with:

- Product Strategy
- Relationships
- Advertising
- Licensing
- Staffing
- Pricing
- Sales

Please use this book to focus and market your product or service through your brand, providing real value and connection with your stakeholders, partners, employees and customers. This is the real reason for branding and used in this way you will be successful.

Branded behavior?

Have you ever paid three dollars for a cup of coffee; more than $30,000 for a new automobile or two, three, four or more dollars, for a bottle of water? If you have, you have already been participating in this 'automagical' behavior of brands, in a predictable, profitable way. Now is the time for you to unscrew the lid from the genie's bottle. Now is the time you get to fully understand the codes, colors, signs and secret signals through which brands communicate regularly, frequently and almost completely unconsciously with humanity.

Understanding on a conscious level does not make brands any less useful or interesting. In fact, your deeper understanding will broaden your understanding of humanity as a whole, and give you great insight to our civilization, culture and whereabouts in the grand scheme of things.

There is lots of ammunition, by way of evidence, suggested in this book— and really; look around! Our culture, and our world is filled with brands, offering us the perfect proving grounds for formulas, hypotheses and theory. Not only this, but we have not only successful brands, but myriad failed brands to study as well. I encourage you to look in your own world for examples, which may make this book not only more relevant, but useful and interesting to you.

Many people (mistakenly) believe that they make only rational, logical purchasing decisions and that therefore all this 'branding business' is a waste of time, money and effort. Nothing could be further from the truth! Almost always the intuitive, emotional side leads in speed of processing and recognition (recall color vs. letter recognition) and then follows us with Rational Justification. 'Oh, I bought this soup because it's a healthier choice,' ignoring the fact the healthiest choice was likely to make your own soup.

We crave instant and easy, and while it may not be laudable, it will likely be some time before we shift as a species from that particular paradigm. In reality, a mixture of emotional and rational go into almost any decision. In branding we are simply recognizing the importance of the emotional and then are employing rational (left brain) tools, arguments and planning to put them into place, knowing our customers will be using the unwitting right brain to make their selection—even while they use their left brain to justify this decision. This is a whole-brain work, folks!

Following are a few of the left-brain reasons businesses invest in branding.

A Baker's Dozen:
13 Business Reasons for Branding

The process of Brand Identification will help uncover which is the most appropriate choice for any brand proposition, and aid in the development and delivery of both correct language and a market solution-set which appeals to the unmet needs (Emotional Gap) of the market being sought.

Branding seeks to make emotional connections between a product, organization or identity and people for a variety of reasons, including:

1. To establish market supremacy;
2. To set apart similar products with a perceptual difference;
3. To distinguish one manufacturer's products from another's;
4. To create new space for a product when markets appear saturated;
5. To engage workforces with energy, spirit or *esprit de corps*;
6. To provide a consistent set of measures of a product or service so that customers can create reliable expectations;
7. To clearly identify real differences in a meaningful way that buyers 'get' without having to understand all the technical details;
8. To aid customers in quickly and easily identifying an 'original' product or service from look-alike or copycat competitors;
9. To provide CEOs and other leaders with a consistent and commonly understood strategy from which to develop tactics;
10. To develop alignment between all stakeholders, uniting mission, values, vision and purpose within a commonly aligned and understood direction
11. To engage sales forces with clarity and common understanding of what makes their products and services distinguished, compared to both the competition, and to alternative solution approaches
12. To unite all aspects of marketing and public relations so that all collateral such as print web and media seem to be 'sung from the same hymnbook', displaying consistency of message and feeling
13. To make more money, more automatically, for longer.

Through analysis we can identify the Question posed by brand, and thereby, the need it fulfills. Knowing this allows us to identify Emotional Gap relating to the Primal Requirement within individuals, which pertain to the Promise the brand delivers on. We use Primal Requirement as a term relative to Maslow's hierarchy of needs, which are centered on a set of relative needs.

As you can see, 'brand' has developed a much more complex, and nuanced definition than the original 'owner's mark' definition. Today it is commonly understood that brands truly exist in the minds and hearts of the people who interact with them. While brands are human constructs, which are synthetically created by their owners, the impressions they create belong to their audience(s)—both internal and external. Frequently, these impressions are quite *dis*similar to what their owners set out to create. (Sometimes better, often worse).

Mostly though, brands simply occur as accidental. For every successful brand in the marketplace there are hundreds, if not thousands of brand casualties. I identify a brand casualty as any brand that does not outlive its founder(s). A typical example might be the neighborhood shoe store that has served for forty of more years—and then, when its owner(s) decide to retire, simply closes up. What a waste! All those thousands of impressions and relationships simply put to death—including the jobs of its employees. On a financial level this is also sad, since the liquidation value of a business will always be less than the value of a business as a 'going concern' – complete with a realistic assessment of its goodwill—i.e. its brand equity.

I do think that succession is one of the most important reasons to brand, and that today the true brand may outlive both its founder and it initial genesis to surpass everyone's expectations and be a genuine human and financial asset.

But, frankly, with a dozen reasons listed, and having your own motivations, I am sure as well, you may likely adapt your own top four or five reasons to participate more fully in branding, now that you are starting to understand its strategic supremacy.

Branding is far and away the fastest route to increased margins, improved market share and a more stable income sheet.

When you really think about it, branding is simply a systematic way of constructing a super consistent business. It's just that the level of systemization and the depth of consistency accessed through branding is deeper than linear thought alone accesses. Brands ask us to look and see both holistically and holographically.

Unspoken Promises
Differentiate Rivals from Competitors

Pepsi and Coke may be arch-rivals, but they are not truly competitors. Let me explain why.

For decades the Coca-Cola company and the Pepsi-Cola company squared off against other, lambasting each other in public, pitting sales territories against sales territories, competing for fast-food, restaurant and quick-serve territory. Both companies make the majority of their sales through restaurants using a very similar formula and distribution method. Concentrated syrup is shipped to restaurants and mixed with carbon dioxide and water through a fountain machine at the point of purchase. In like manner, canned and bottle versions of product are distributed through grocery channels in again, very like format and similar price.

Here's the thing, however. Brands actually compete on two, distinctly different levels. It is important to notice both before rushing to judgment (or to action) as you will see. The first level of competition is one we are all familiar with because it is so obvious. This is the place of category. On the level of category, Coke and Pepsi ARE clearly rivals, both selling a carbonated water-based sweet caffeinated cola-flavored beverage. Got it. The second level however, is both subtler AND more powerful. Ignoring this other level can have devastating consequences. I'll show you two.

This second level is the level of persona. This is the level where emotion comes in. On this level you will learn that Pepsi and Coke are not really rivals, nor even competitors at all. Coke's Palace persona promise is "forever" while Pepsi's Hotel promise is "transformation". Could there be two more different promises?

1. When I choose Coke, I'm saying I like things the way they are.
2. When I choose Pepsi, I'm saying I'm up for a change.

Two more dramatically different mind-sets, and philosophies can hardly be said to exist. If you ignore the competition at the level of the persona there are two huge mistakes waiting to happen:

1. You may be duped into thinking that your apparent competitors' strategy is superior and start playing their game (which you will never be able to win, by definition, as it is their game).
2. In your present myopia you may completely miss a new real competitor; (Red Bull anyone?) and let them establish a toe-hold you've been ignoring, which can rapidly become a wedge between you and your core audience.

Both of these are hegemonic mistakes, which is to say mistakes made by having a faulty underlying belief structure. Segmenting brands by archetype, instead of or in addition to by product category, prevents this fundamental misunderstanding of how brands and competition work together to segment emotional gap on a population-wide basis through use of basic human psychology.

Through complacency, long-standing brands are frequently the ones to be duped in such a way. There are too many cases to make a complete list, from Xerox (fax machines and email) on down. In the bottled beverage area, Pepsi and Coke have both allowed themselves to be duped, one by the other, then by an outsider at different times.

Smaller businesses can make this mistake as well, so look out for this in your own category—and your unspoken promise zone.

Rivals, not competitors?

Duopoly succeeds by monopolizing the market conversation and hunkering down on existing standards. Coke and Pepsi have done this super successfully for decades. The first product was the elimination of alternative choices from the market conversation, focusing instead on an alternate BRAND conversation. So, instead of cola, root beer or orange soda, it was Coke or Pepsi (cola). This marginalization of 'everything else' is hegemonic to brand isolationism and efficiencies of scale frequently required for global infrastructure.

BASICALLY, we received the message through MASSIVE amounts of media that we NEED to know whether we like Coke or Pepsi MORE. The fact that both of these are virtually identical to each other, or that there are hundreds of other, really different things we could like, from Sprite to mineral water, to meditating on a lotus flower was irrelevant. Or, to be more accurate, is relevant only in a cost-saving way to the brands, which cooperate on everything from core content (cola) to can and bottle sizes, reaping vast efficiencies, in doing so.

It's hard to overestimate the sheer volume of business and wealth this has accrued either group. By effectively marginalizing all other beverage conversations, Coke and Pepsi set a standard of expectation for generations. In so doing they built two of the largest brands in the world, including what was until recently the number one brand by value worldwide; Coca-Cola.

The thing we have to remember, as creative branders, is that people are out there seeking emotional solutions—not necessarily carbonated beverages. If they are seeking both, then there may be up to seven different ways to approach them. Since the Palace and Hotel channels are 'full', then introducing another competitor on either of these channels seems like a challenge.

A new competitor in the area of carbonated caffeinated beverages would probably be well-served to choose one of the five formulas not in use when introducing a product so that he was not competing for the same emotions that Coke and Pepsi already have locked up—but the market is not always rational, as we shall see.

Quantum Branding?

While it may appear that we are inundated with an infinite volume of brand messages day and day out, in actuality, we have a quite finite limit to the number of messages we can "onboard" through our bilateral in-built fuzzy-logic analysis systems (that's body and brain to most people).

Since we clearly have finite capacity for the number of things we can keep track of or even know about, brands effectively compete for our attention in different fields, or categories, of attention.

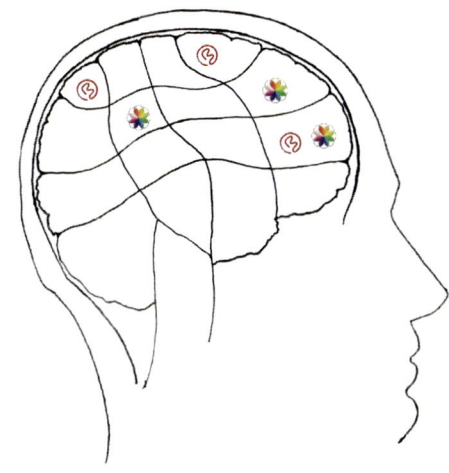

Our attention may be counted in one of two different ways, depending on how we consider it, kind of like quantum events. Quantum events can be observed as particles or as waves, depending on perspective. The perspective chosen influences the result. This has transformed our view of physics, and how we view the world.

Today the popular conversation is no longer about soft-drinks. Today's question is iPhone versus Android. Here again, we are duped into thinking that the two prominent choices represent choice. Again, the 'choice' is between, essentially two carbonated water-based sweet caffeinated cola-flavored beverages, er 1970s-interface driven smartphones, and we NEED to know which we like MORE.

Hold the phone, yet, though. Did we not just say Coke and Pepsi didn't compete on category, yet on emotion; right! Apple and Android also compete on emotion, meaning that die-hard fans of one of the other rarely switch loyalties mid-stream. This serves to focus and concentrate the conversation on the existing sweet-stuff—the world of downloadable apps, equivalent to Coke's (and Pepsi's) caffeine-sugar rush dose. We come back again and again for that sugar rush and have to deal with the aftereffect of spiking insulin and attention levels for hours afterword.

Today, the number one brand in the world is Apple, which displaced Coke a few years back. And Google? Number two.

We all understand the difference between sugary beverages and smartphones, but do we understand the difference between the emotional promises made by the different brands?

We must, if we are to really get how the real economics work, beyond the 'Disneyland scale' we are presented with through media, advertising and industry.

So far, we see that brands occur for at least a dozen reasons, differentiate themselves from competitors based on unspoken categorical promises, are holistic, and may occur as quantum entities, that is, they take on meaning depending on the observer.

In the chapter that that follows, I outline the necessity of emotional gap in creating brand identification. From this it will become clear there is an overall Gestalt to brands, explained in the next chapter following.

Below, costumed dancer makes her entrance at a branded promotional fund-raising event in Toronto, Canada. Artistic Direction by the Author.

Emotional Gap Source of Brand Identification

Every one of the brands in the Matriarchy of Brands resonates on a specific wave-length or frequency and each one answers a different unspoken question, with a unique unspoken promise.

Following is a chart showing all seven kinds with their primal requirement listed (this relates to Maslow) and they psychological domain, as well as their primal question along with their unspoken promise.

Specific Brand Types and Promises

Arche-type	Primal Requirement	Psychological Domain	Unspoken Question	Unspoken Promise
House	Sexual Fecundity	Happiness	What?	More, For Less
Tower	Sexual Attractiveness	Popularity	Who?	You, Only Better
Bridge	Self-expression	Liberty	Why?	Adventure, Because You Can
Hotel	Freedom	Identity	Which?	Your Choice, Here & Now
Castle	Survival	Security	Where?	Safety, Everywhere
Palace	Life	Time	When?	Forever, Immortality
Theater	Community	Family	How?	Together

It is ALL about emotional 'gap'.

Since there are only a limited number of emotional wavelengths for brands to communicate on, it often serves brands to 'irritate' the 'gap' in our happiness to exploit places where we feel less than fully expressed, attracting us to them.

With just seven historic emotional 'channels' that brands communicate their salvation, er solutions, along, many brands may be competing for these limited areas of attention. With every brand on the Interbrand 100 conforming to one of these seven behavioral 'types' and therefore delivering one of seven emotional salvations for gaps in human behavior, understanding or being. In this way, their marketing messages penetrate the deluge facing us in such a way that a small yet significant number penetrate and activate so strongly that it is virtually impossible to make one's way in today's world—your modern life—without being profoundly impacted with at least several of these brands every single day.

Brands close Emotional Gaps within certain Psychological Domains with Unspoken Promises. Following is a chart relating Primal Requirements to specific Psychological Domains, Unspoken Questions and Unspoken Promises.

The end goal of all marketing is Brand Identification—that is the identification of a brand with an individual. Therefore, beginning with the end in mind, it is valuable to first define and examine this goal in some detail prior to evaluating any plans within the marketplace. Three questions surely need to be addressed:

1. What does the process of identification look like?
2. Who are the individuals in question?
3. Finally, what is the purpose of branding and what can we say about a specific brand's nature?

We say we identify with someone when we have a sense of relatedness with him or her. Webster defines identification as a mental mechanism wherein the individual gains gratification, emotional support, or relief from anxiety by attributing to himself consciously or unconsciously the characteristics of another person or group; or orientation of the self in regard to something with a resulting feeling of close emotional association.

With regard to a brand, therefore, identification occurs when an individual gains gratification, emotional support or relief from anxiety through a brand experience; or orients him/herself to it with a feeling of close emotional association. Since emotion is involved as this occurs, logic is surpassed and choices may freely be made without prejudice to prior experiences, preferences, or even pre-existing knowledge.

An individual with strong brand identification will make purchasing decisions based on "gut feeling", "instinct", "because I need it" or any number of other reasons he or she may come up with (including logical ones they develop after the fact), which justify their preference. The goal of brand identification is to implant a strong emotional preference for a brand over all competing entities.

Weak or poor brand identification is extremely costly to an organization because while an individual may make a purchasing decision once or a few times based purely on ration—or upon a personal relationship—these causes can never be systemic (around all the time) and may easily be overcome by more powerful emotional identification reasons from a competing brand (i.e. brand identification).

Brand identification makes sense as a primary marketing goal because individual who identify with a brand are not easily swayed from their choice—it is a truism in sales that people decide emotionally, and then justify their decisions rationally.

The individuals involved in brand identification are internal, intermediate, and external.

The most crucial (and oft ignored) faction of individuals is internal. Owners, partners, directors, franchisees, employees, and subcontractors (i.e. anyone who depends day to day on the functioning of the brand) need to be able to identify with the brand for the brand to present coherent and functional communication with others. Failure in this area will inevitably result in marketplace failure because ultimately service delivery is completed by people; if the people involved do not identify with the brand then others will not either. Further action will be a non-starter—therefore in developing brand identification we devote significant energies to internal individuals first.

The next most important group of individuals is intermediate. Suppliers, customers, strategic partners and sponsors are the lifeblood of day-to-day business. With strong brand identification, these individuals will present a loyal band of followers, supporting ongoing market action and growth. Without brand identification this group is more akin to a group of wandering nomads. Here today, gone tomorrow.

Finally, external individuals may be solicited into the brand identification process. These individuals feed off the enthusiasm of internal and intermediate groups and are a source of growth for the contingents of internal and intermediate individuals. Creating the opportunity for Brand Identification for members from the general public is the object of many, if not most, marketing campaigns. In an efficient and effectively branded organization it is the natural progression and logical outcome from all other activities—not an end in itself.

Successful brand identification occurs first with internal individuals and concludes later with members of the general public. Now that we can prioritize brand identification we may well ask some interesting questions of branding, and of the brand's nature.

Since brand identification is clearly a powerful market force, a natural question arises: what causes an individual to identify with a brand? Another way to pose this question: why would an individual emotionally involve him/herself with an incorporate entity other than another individual (i.e. a besides human relationship)?

Emotional Gap Provides Space for Emotional Identification

The reason for developing an emotional identification with a brand or company is to fulfill emotional requirements that are not being met through other (human and or corporate) relationships. An emotional gap between need and fulfillment must exist for brand identification to develop.

The reasons for a gap existing are as numerous as the individuals facing them—but one thing is common—a requirement for emotional fulfillment which is not being satisfactorily met through other forms of relatedness. The forms of emotional non-fulfillment are numerous, but in terms of fulfillment by brands these may be reduced to a handful of primal requirements or desires which represent continuums within the human condition.

From every (unfulfilled) emotional requirement we can derive a psychological domain, or reference area. For instance, the primal requirement for sexual attractiveness relates to the psychological domain of popularity. These, in turn, relate to fundamental, or basic questions we all ask—the brand returns an answer—or more fundamentally, a Promise. The question posed by the psychological domain of Popularity is *Who?*. The unspoken promise is *You, Only Better*. In this manner, brands deliver an emotionally satisfying response to nearly all emotional gaps in the human condition.

Brands work by contrasting the painful emotional identification between the 'something missing' for the individual with the implicit delivery within the unspoken promise by the brand. Individuals respond emotionally, expressed by spending money and or making other 'branded' transactions, like talking about or recommending the brand to others.

Brands alter behaviors by introducing new concepts through solutions bathed in light of an unvarying unspoken promise that resonates with on-going needs of the individual. Emotional needs trump many far more practical desires and so inform the brand economy.

This is a time to realize how the precise mechanism works of emotional gap works and why it is vital to brand identification, plus how to exploit it in your organization. Failure to do so will be met by the forces of competition and contest inevitably including others willing to spend their way to success. Best to avoid race to the bottom contests and succeed on your promise, away from where other competition exists, where you may establish your own brand vortex, value and proposition.

Gestalt of It All: How Brands Are Holistic

Gestalt is a nineteenth century word we inherit from German. The meaning in English is most commonly used as a psychological term. A central idea of Gestalt psychology is the mind forms a whole, a Gestalt that has a reality separate from, and greater than its parts.

The original famous phrase of Gestalt psychologist Kurt Koffka, "The whole is other than the sum of the parts" is often incorrectly translated as "The whole is greater than the sum of its parts" and thus used when explaining gestalt theory, and further incorrectly applied to systems theory. Koffka did not like the translation. He firmly corrected students who replaced "other" by "greater". "This is not a principle of addition" he said. The whole has an independent existence.

Holism is a term that arose around the same term, with Greek origins, via South Africa. Holism holds that natural systems and their properties should be held as wholes, not as collections of parts. In other words, by examining a spark plug, you will not be able to understand, or necessarily deduce an internal combustion engine.

It is important to have a grasp of these two concepts, for brands function very much as natural systems, and even like a mind. The artificial separation between brand components and the didactic language that is most often applied to business theory, especially to sales, marketing and finance is especially cumbersome to enabling any real understanding of brand function. The idea that branding **is** marketing, or *even* that branding is more relevant to marketing than it is to, let us say, Human Resources, is really backwards, if not downright objectionable.

Let us examine this idea. We have identified that: *A brand is the set of relationships through which a commercial, organizational or product identity connects with people.* So, how can branding be about marketing, if it is not (first) about the people inside the organization? There's only one way, and that is if the branding is applied as icing over top of the company and its product. In other words, if the company feels it is all right to have one set of set of relationships inside a company, and another type of ideals externally. While we all understand that this is a commonplace event, it is anathema to successful branding. You cannot build or maintain a successful brand in the economy that is based on this sort of loose moral footing. Enron, anyone?

I like the word gestalt, as a simile to brand, for the definition is that the mind is *greater* than the sum of its parts. This implies not only that is it impractical to approach branding from its constituent articles (i.e. slogans, tactics, media and graphical concepts) but that this approach will never achieve as great a result as beginning with the overall strategy: the big picture must win out. The idea of Coca-Cola is not just to sell a sweetened carbonated beverage in concentrate form to franchised bottlers. Neither is it a swirling white logo on a red can. Nor is it a bottle shape. It is none of these just as it is all of these—and more.

When discussing brand strategy, I often use the terms 'feel', 'flavor' as well as 'on-code' and 'off-code'. These are shortcut phrases to get across bigger concepts that relate to both holism and Gestalt. I will often notice that something 'doesn't quite feel right' about a brand, when I am asked to audit one. At first, exactly what this may be might not be precisely apparent; because all that is noticeable is that certain elements are not meshing well together, or gelling to form a (greater) whole. Frequently (usually in fact) there are more than three variables "out of synch", which tends to be instantly identifiable (to me) as nothing more than 'not tasting right'. With careful analysis, however I am always able to discern what the 'correct' flavor is, within a given context.

Imagine you are making soup and you ask somebody to taste it. You tell her it is tomato soup, but to her the flavor of tomatoes is not present, only celery, lobster and cream. She will have some time to discover what is missing—or should not be present, if you really want tomato soup! Perhaps tomato soup was a concept you had in mind this morning, but this afternoon when you began cooking, you opened the cookbook to lobster bisque and started there, instead. As a tester, "does this seem like tomato soup?" is on her mind. How can this be saved? A different name, *brand* for your soup is in order.

At the end of the day, elements are, technically either 'on-code' or 'off-code'. Since we are dealing with a holistic structure, we can say definitively that ham does not belong in a vegetarian goulash recipe! The ham is 'off-code' and must be excised. Otherwise, the goulash is not vegetarian and therefore, could not be served with any sort of integrity. Eventually, this would come back with some very furious vegetarian diners. In addition, you may find the cook does not enjoy being lambasted by his customers! On the other hand, paprika is a traditional spice with Hungarian cuisine, the original source of Goulash, so in our vegetarian variation might be very much 'on-code'—if it contributes to an overall 'Vegetarian-Goulashness' of the completed dish.

In this chapter, we use Chanel as an example company to illustrate both the concepts of Gestalt, and holism. Chanel has many signature design elements, some well-known, others not as much so, each of which contributes to the 'Chanelness' of Chanel. Here are a few examples:

1. Double interlocking 'CC' logo
2. Diamond-pattern quilting on handbags and other items
3. Tweed, 'English country-style' suits for women
4. Back of skirt weighted with a small chain
5. White silk camellias
6. Chunky, oversize costume jewelry
7. Chain link handles with leather braided into chain
8. Stylized diamond square-cut shape, i.e. No. 5 bottle top
9. Black and white, or gold-colored logo
10. Mirrors

There are many (many) more. Could you throw all these together and achieve 'Chanel'? No. As the founder and spiritual head, Coco Chanel, famously declared: "Simplicity is the keynote of all true elegance." One of the reasons that Chanel was, and is perennially successful, is that it functions holistically as a company, and the concept of Gestalt is always present in the look, achieved whereby 'the sum is greater than the parts' i.e. simplicity! One of my greatest lessons in Chanel styling was to always accessorize, and then remove one or two items. The individual components were almost always so strong that less was, indeed, more.

Nor was this idea of 'the look' confined to the products. As I mentioned, Chanel managers—indeed all retail employees are clothed in Chanel. And, the stores are impeccably designed to reflect the same ethos, as is all packaging, advertising and visual collateral. A job at Chanel is a job for life, perfectly expressing in real business terms the quality of timelessness for which the brand is so well-known.

Why is this important? In addition to being a fashion mainstay, Chanel is one of the top 100 brands in the world—meaning of the millions and millions of companies out there it is consistently one 100 brightest, most visible and *profitable* names in the world!

Holism does not necessarily come easily, or cheaply. But if you want your brand to deliver on your unspoken promise, you had better start figuring out what is your Gestalt: exactly how is your brand greater than its parts? What are your keynote aspects? And what philosophy 'puts it all together' a la Coco Chanel's "Simplicity is the keynote of all true elegance."

In March of 1997 when I was the Vice-President of the Display Guy Retail Design Co, the fastest growing and highest volume regional window display and retail merchandising firm in Canada. On a Wednesday morning the local CHANEL boutique manager called me at and requested an interview: my brand intuition kicked into overdrive! Although I did not know it quite as much at that time, I felt intuitively this was a very important connection, and discussion. Of course, I did know something of CHANEL's history. But being a child of the 70s, I thought of it as company with perfume and a few gaudy, chunky-looking accessories. I was aware of the beautiful, classic signature designs of CHANEL's perfumes, based on the most classic of all, CHANEL No. 5.

While having an intimate understanding of some Department Store purchased fragrances on my Mother's dresser, I was not aware of the long and storied history of Coco Chanel the couturier and how she came to change the way women dress, and the very fashion industry. Nevertheless, I certainly felt that meeting the local CHANEL manager was an occasion to put on my best suit and tie, which I did the day I went to meet her. If you have ever been in a couture shop, or a retail outlet of a company that produces couture, you will be aware there is certain hushed quality to such places. Everything is just a bit special!

CHANEL's Vancouver store was very small, probably only about 1,000 square feet, but everything about it was designed and built 'just so' to maximize every centimeter of space. The moment I arrived, this was obvious. From the door handles, which were shaped like the lids of Chanel perfume bottles, to the liveried doorman, who opened the door, there was an immediate impression of wealth, status and elegance. Inside, the entire store was decorated like a museum or gallery. Every single vertical surface was either delicately smoked mirror, or black lacquer. The layout was as precisely designed as a doll's house, you could not be quite sure of its dimensions or layout until you were used to it. In the back, I met with the manager in her office, which was unlike other store manager's offices I had seen. Most of these doubled as staff rooms, frequently piled high with boxes, hangers and often equipped with odds and ends of mechanical equipment like water heaters and wash up sinks. Colette's office had none of that. Everything was built-in. The same calm hush that pervaded the retail area also dominated in her office, like the thick, pale plush carpet. Comfortable office chairs and European-looking computer terminals completed the furnishings. "So this was how the other half lives," I remember thinking.

Collette was an elegant, middle-aged French-Canadian woman attired at all times, head to toe in CHANEL, including just the right chunky jewelry. I later learned she had a generous clothing allowance. She was all strictly professional and straight to business. "I need someone to do my windows," she announced. "Edgar can't do them any longer, and he recommended your company." That's direct, I thought. At the same time, I thought, wow Edgar recommended Display Guy; and "Excellent! A true prestige customer who will provide us with an excellent reference and who can afford our best work."

I put together a proposal, which she somewhat grudgingly accepted on my second visit, making changes to the contract (nobody has ever done that, I told her—to which she replied, "this clause is not acceptable to CHANEL, I won't have it." End of discussion. Therefore, CHANEL was our only customer which did not have the customary square purple "Display Guy" logo discreetly placed on a lower corner of the window.

Proudly, I returned to the office to let my staff know the good news! We had the most prestigious boutique in Vancouver as a client! The next job was to select the team members to service this client. Because CHANEL used mannequins, and we only had one staff member, Ken, with real fashion mannequin experience. I sent him with a junior to assist. I thought they would feel honored. Boy was I wrong!

After the first day of merchandising, at CHANEL I was eager to hear how it went. Clearly something was up. Ken was in one of his moods.

I asked chirpily: "How did it go?"

"Very difficult," he replied.

"Why?"

"Not only do we have to wear all black, but there's no room to move things around. She's very fussy and there aren't any props to work with. It's really stressful."

Maybe things will sort themselves out, I thought. After a couple more visits, it clearly wasn't working out. I was stressed. No one else has mannequin experience, I'd tried two different assistants and it didn't seem to make a difference. All my staff felt stressed and hassled by what I thought was a prestige job and an honor to work with such a beautiful, elegant and storied brand.

Finally, I decided I had to do something, but without any real answer in mind, I called Collette and made an appointment for the next day. I met her again, but this time with real heaviness in my heart. I had to tell her we could not fulfill her contract. Not only would I be giving up a lucrative guaranteed monthly income, but all the prestige that went with it! I told her the bad news:

"We don't have any staff members who can do the work to our mutual satisfaction, I'm sorry, but I don't see any solution."

"What about you?" Collette responded, quickly, crisply and business-like as usual.

"ME?" I cried, "I don't do merchandising, and I have never worked with mannequins; I run the company, that's my job." Even while I said it, I knew there was hollowness to my words.

"You will do just fine," she said, "you understand the brand, everything else you may learn!"

To my delight, she was right! I loved merchandising at CHANEL. I liked wearing all black. It didn't bother me in the least there was very little space to work in, I like to stay neat and organized. The merchandise was so beautiful very little was required to make it shine—usually less and less; then pin-point precise lighting, which was a forte of mine. Brand is paramount.

Nevertheless, my first day of creating a window display at CHANEL *was* nerve-wracking. Not only was it my first display for the most prestigious store in my city, but it was the first window display I had ever done by myself!

I labored all morning positioning two mannequins plus some very simple props and three or four handbags. After about three hours of this I felt a bit exhausted and not at all satisfied with the results. But: what more could I do? I went and asked Collette to review my work. She came outside and looked at my window display. First, she cocked her head one way, chin in hand; then, the other. At last, she spoke:

"What do YOU think?" she asked, looking at my quizzically.

"I'm not sure about this," I said pointing at one element.

"Try moving it," she said. I did, and she said it was fine and that was that.

In that moment I understood it was all about feeling, and that love for the brand is paramount. Since I really knew all the rules of display, specifically since I had a technical background with lighting and color, the rest was actually just a test of confidence.

I never required her advice again and I never sweated it afterwards. I headed visuals for CHANEL Vancouver for two more years, and it was my only 'hands-on' client, until I expanded my career, leaving behind Vancouver and the first half of my career. During those two years I loved my twice a month visits to the boutique and always looked forward to my 'CHANEL days'. I was happy there.

At Collette's request, I had some of my own interpretations of the Paris prop designs implemented, as I felt they were more appropriate to this store and managed to save the store local budget; while providing useful local employment in Vancouver to our team of local artisans. These kinds of jobs kept five or six staff busy full-time at Display Guy Retail Design Co. for a few most creative years in the late 90s. These were good times.

Theater Brands, like Display Guy, can create outsize impressions—and profits, while having fun in the process!

Many of my warmest work and career experiences came from my time helping Display Guy become one of the largest merchandising firms in Canada*. We had an amazing team and I stay in touch with many of them.

On-screen host introduces Display Guy video. Highlights include, walking legs (above), pedaling invisible bike rider on real mountain bike (below). Client testimonials played between example footage of our unique window displays. The client below is explaining how they have found no need for any other advertising. Effectively brand-integrated promotions can be exceptionally effective.

After five years in one location, one client reported getting a 43% increase in month-to-month sales immediately following the start of theater-style promotions in the front two feet of his store. Needless to say, this client, and most others, had no hesitation in signing multiple annual contracts.

* At the time: 20th century.

Brand Identification: How Brands Work

Brand development is a century-proven method to build long-lasting, high value, innovative and productive companies. How can the power of this big business proven high-output economic motor be harnessed in day to day practice?

Organizations today frequently involve complex layers of bureaucracy—siloed inefficiencies throughout many sections and parts of organization. The wonder of it is that the whole system functions at all—let alone well. Due in part to the efficiency gap (which is significant—say in the seventy to ninety percent range) economic cracks are beginning to show. There is room for improvement.

Brand identification is the unrecognized work horse of the economy. Anyone who has tried to go grocery shopping in a foreign country knows how difficult it is to efficiently conduct a normal series of transactions, a "shopping list" of concerns; for instance, a can of Campbell's Tomato Soup, a six-pack of Coke and some Bryer's Ice Cream. We know what we are seeking—we do not even have to say the words. A can of Campbell's soup is pretty easy to recognize. Finding familiar soup in Nepal or Ireland is not as easy—without the benefit of brand identification life slows to a crawl.

We brand everything that we think of. We just do not normally think of it that way. But when we know not to expect that sort of remark from "Mom" then we are essentially saying this behavior is not congruent with our Mother—we are essentially saying we know what "Mom" would talk about, and how. Not necessarily true—but we act as if this is the truth. Other times, it may be just an image, a look, a color, or a smell—the smell of your kitchen, which you unconsciously associate (i.e. brand) with "home".

Witness the power of our minds! We categorize so efficiently. Sometimes we are hasty to disregard our first impressions perhaps considering them offensive or derogatory—but listen less to your censor and more to the value these impressions are giving you for the vast amounts of information, not to say knowledge, we can conjure upon a name, an image, or a smell.

A brand is a story. It is not contracts, buildings, inventory, cash or loans—or even logos or catch-phrases. It is simply a story which circulates in people's minds.

In 2008 the number one category was still Bottled Beverages and the number one story was Coca-Cola. From start-up it took Coca-Cola approximately fifty years to achieve this status. In the current climate it is possible to establish a new global category, and brand preference within it, much more quickly. To achieve this, emerging enterprise must offer distinctly different product choices.

While there are thousands of brands with global aspirations, there are truly only a handful of top-level key mind-space categories. These unspoken areas of popular emotional gap relate to areas of fundamental human aspiration and relate to ordinary-language questions such as 'who?', 'what?', or 'where?'.

Top brands respond to the questions in mind-space with extraordinary (unstated) Answers and beyond those (archetypal) Promises. For instance, the question in the mind-space area of 'who?' is answered with the answer 'you, only better.' Beyond this is the archetypal promise of 'popularity'. Starbucks has become very successful by mining this previously under-developed area of mind-space. In the space of a few years Starbucks has become a global brand with brand valuation of almost four billion dollars (exceeding hard assets), by dominating the Tower (green) area of mind-space (i.e. Who?).

Known Characteristics of Brand Archetypes

Let us examine some of the characteristics of brand archetypal personality that are common to all types.

1. Gender. Brand archetypes have a gender and a sexual preference.
2. Color. All brand archetypes refer to a color, or set of colors.
3. Smell. All brand archetypes have a scent, smell or odor.
4. Form. All brand archetypes have a general form or shape.
5. Promise. All brand archetypes carry with them a specific and certain promise. This is called the unspoken promise.
6. Price. All brand archetypes carry with them guidelines for comparison pricing.
7. Promotion. All brand archetypes have a certain set of ideal promotional characteristics.

What does archetype NOT inform? Archetype does not determine the specific name of your brand, or shade of color. It doesn't distinguish the precise scent mixture, nor exact logo form or shape. Nor does archetype determine your fixed price point or your next month's promotion. In fact, there is just one aspect that is always pretty much identical, and that is Promise. Each archetype carries with it one unspoken promise, and this promise, being unspoken, may be, and in fact is, identical to brands that conform to that one type.

So far, we have determined that archetype will help us through identification of a number of strategic aspects of brand development and execution and this is designed to make our jobs both easier and more effective within the marketplace.

We have also noted that there is a singular aspect to brand archetype that is both central and predetermined. This aspect is promise. While we do not say 'a brand is a promise' we do know all real brands hold a promise. And we know this promise, being unspoken, is secret.

How can a secret promise hold value for our brand? Secrets hold enormous power and appeal. Remember the first time you were told a secret—or learned that someone you knew had one. What was your reaction? Did you want to know the secret? Did you pass it on? Did you keep it a secret? There is something almost magical about secrets that holds endless fascination. The unspoken promise of every successful brand is just such a magnet. While the brand does not likely refer to their secret (we are not talking about the Caramilk secret, or Coke's secret formula—although these are both laudable marketing gimmicks), the brand does infer a secret through the coding of its communications. There is one underlying, singular premise held within the secret, unspoken promise, around which all communications must revolve. This premise, when understood by the *cognoscenti* (that would be you) will provide endless ammunition for the creative development and execution of your communications.

How does our audience relate to or even know about the unspoken promise? Simple: there is an unspoken *question* posed by the listener (to the brand) that the unspoken *promise* provides an automatic response to. The power of the hidden question/hidden answer is that both of these occur on an unconscious level, automatically, in response to other cues, such as color, form and price.

Unspoken questions are mainly single word 'W' questions, such as When? Where? and What? Unspoken promises that counter them are broad and categorical, like Forever! Everywhere! And More Loving for Less.

Though both these queries and answers are not directly stated, they present themselves as themes, which underlie all communications. They are the background, or wallpaper to the brand environment, just out of focal range, but context-setting, and therefore decisive, nevertheless.

Knowing and understanding your unspoken promise is the single greatest point of leverage you will possess in your brand arsenal. Remember, your brand communicates effectively only by communicating at all levels, and with one message. This message is the same for you, your stakeholders, employees, partners and customers. Therefore, there really is only one product you must deliver: your unspoken promise is the ultimate quality checkpoint for your brand. Look at any transaction, communication, marketing piece or sales conversation. Does it deliver or does it conflict with your unspoken promise? It really is that simple. Devote time and effort to truly digging into your brand's unspoken promise and understand it on a deep, deep level.

Government Efficiency

September 2005. Government was the last possible place I ever thought I would be working, I thought to myself as I pressed the number nine in the glass and brushed steel elevator. Yet here I was, about to start a contract at the Alberta Ministry of Restructuring and Government Efficiency. Parenthetically, I wandered what it all meant.

Here was the lunchroom, this is the Director of such and such, that is the Deputy Minister's office, this is the Assistant Deputy Minister of infrastructure, this is her assistant, and so on. At the first meeting I attended, there were so many acronyms and titles flying around, that I had zero idea what the meeting had been about.

Back at my desk, in a solid, window-facing cubicle beside a vast array of empty cubicles I came back to the subject at hand. I had been brought on board ostensibly for my event design and production experience. Recently transplanted from Toronto, this was a position in Edmonton, city of my birth—the self-same place that four years earlier I had been shamelessly promoting Benson and Hedges cigarettes.

The environment could not have been a greater contrast. Whereas the B&H folks were partiers, most people around here looked like they had never been to a party—and like they needed to, as well! My direct supervisor Shawna, was a nervous, high-strung woman who made a point that she had an MBA in Human Resources, and that she had been recruited from another province. I found her likeable, but rule-bound.

In three weeks, the ministry would be having its annual employee get together—850 employees. The date was about all that was set. No venue was booked, no committee organized, and not a sign of a theme in sight. Shawna was concerned that I get the nametags printed. As this seemed to me to be the very least of our troubles, I assured her they would be done, then proceeded onto bigger tasks.

What would the outcome of this event be? When this ministry was formed, recently cobbled together from a bunch of other ministry departments just under a year ago it seems no one had really taken much to heart what precisely it stood for. The standardized employee survey indicated as much—with an employee populace that was dismally unhappy and disengaged. Although I was located in the executive offices where people had 'important work' to do, even there it felt like a morgue, with row on row of empty stations. (Meanwhile, I was to learn later that other areas of the Ministry, located at a dozen different buildings about town, were desperately overcrowded, as well as overworked).

Most of all, I wondered what executive really wanted. I highly doubted their top priority was filling in nametags! Fortunately, my senior boss, the Executive Director of Human Resources, had her office relatively nearby. Friendly and pleasingly corpulent, Luna seemed to take a genuine interest. As well, I learned that she had the direct ear of Peter, the Deputy Minister (government speak for President of the Ministry). Luna came into my area a couple of days after I started.

"There's a new movement in Human Resources that Peter is very interested in," she started out.

"Oh?" I inquired.

"It's about Organizational Values. Organizations want to know what their people's values are. Maybe you could find out something about this."

With that, following a few minor pleasantries, she left, leaving me thinking. My first thought? Thank you! My next thought? What was she talking about and how could I deliver on it?

Next door, in the Ministry of Innovation and Science was a Ph.D. candidate with a kindred mind. Andrew had actually written a paper on the topic, and also referred me to a couple of online articles. Essentially, this relatively new area of organizational development (Values) was being espoused as an indispensable ally in running companies. Through having defined and agreed upon values for the organization, managers would be able to make decisions that were congruent with the direction of the organization.

Later, I was able to place Values within the existing hegemony of corporate discovery that included Mission and Vision, like this:

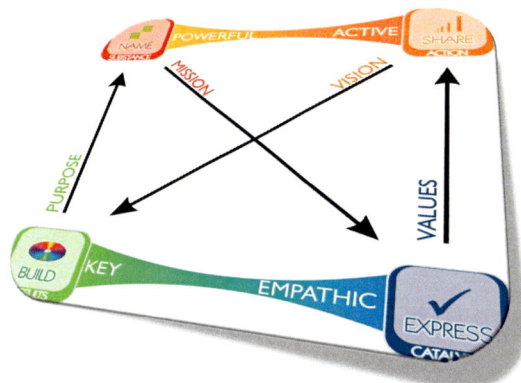

In other words, Values connects in between Mission and Vision. It is through Values that the Mission (what we do) is translated into Vision (where we are going). Why? Values explain HOW we do things. Having clear Values is a critical 'litmus test' in decision-making. Does this proposal connect with our values? If it is in conflict with them, then it is not a right path.

Meanwhile, back at the Alberta Ministry of Restructuring and Government Efficiency, time was ticking. I had gone ahead and booked the venue for the event, since the date was chosen and the only room large enough in town was the Convention Centre. But, other than that, besides my one brief conversation with Luna, everything was pretty much a 'tabula rasa'. Next cubicle to mine, Shawna kept poking her head over the divider to 'see how things are coming'. Usually she saw me reclined in my chair, leaning back from my desk, hands behind my head, eyes half closed. I will give her credit and say that no kittens were birthed on the ninth floor at that time—but it was close for a few days.

Finally, I emerged from my meditation. It was a clear case of organizational branding and this was a stellar opportunity to put many of theories into practice. Typing quickly, I put together a few sentences and a short list and brought it over to Shawna.

"Here's what we need to do," I announced.

Following is a re-creation:

RESTRUCTURING
AND GOVERNMENT
EFFICIENCY

Attn: Senior Manager of Corporate Human Resources
Ministry of Restructuring and Government Efficiency

From Bryce Winter, Corporate Liaison

Dear Shawna:

Here's my plan. As you know we don't have a lot of time, but
I'm confident with the resources outlined we will have no
trouble delivering on a stellar employee event next month:

Community Action League: Develop an action league of 5-8
interested managers able to meet twice a week, in addition to
allocating dedicated time to the event plan, and the event.

Deploy a game mechanism during the event with a bingo-like
paper input mechanism to allow free-form entries into
determining the Ministry's Values.

I recommend that you assist in selecting committee
members, as I do not know the people around the office yet.
I've booked meeting room 917B tomorrow at 1:30 for the
first meeting.

Sincerely,
Bryce Winter

The next day, I had my six junior managers at the meeting. I explained
what we were up to, and then assigned four different planning 'tracks' to
the group. Each track would assemble its own network of 'volunteers' to
follow through on tasks. Finally, I asked the group to develop a name for
itself, and possibly for the event itself.

Since the traditional route was to go outside to an agency to do this sort of
work, this landed a bit uncomfortably at first, for it seems no one had
asked any employees of the Ministry such a thing before. And, wasn't this
a bit unimportant, when we had such important and urgent work to get
done? After a little group facilitation, however, I managed to land the
importance of this first, crucial step. Here is the name and logo, that the

group developed for themselves, the event, and what became an on-going initiative:

Through the experience of co-organizing the event, we developed a great small group that actively 'owned' producing the employee event. And, through mechanisms developed through my company, MARKBRAND GROUP, we were able to tease information, using a fun game-like format, from each individual onto 'bingo' cards, which were collected at the end of the day.

While there is a place for agencies to develop exterior branding work, including polished-looking professional collateral materials, it is my frequent experience that this expensive process, as had been applied at the ministry of Restructuring and Government Efficiency, produces mixed results. The corporate logo for the ministry had the letters RGE artistically displayed under a stylized map of the region in cool tones. Unfortunately, the acronym RGE was pronounced as 'rage' within the Ministry, describing the general consensus of opinion about its structure and formation from separate undesirable 'poor' units of the general government.

In contrast, the 'Better Together' initiative with its homey name and logo and traditional colors was distinctly not 'store bought' looking. This resonated with employees who saw themselves, not an advertising agency, reflected in the initiative.

By utilizing the large labor pool available through Corporate Human Resources for a couple days following the event, we had the hand-written information from the bingo cards input into an Excel spreadsheet. Next, using a thesaurus-like method, I was able to concentrate hundreds of written-in phrases into six main 'Gestalt' themes. These, I presented in a brief report to Executive, the week following the event.

Normally, in governments everywhere, decisions are made slowly and wheels turn at a glacial pace. This time, however, due to the format of the information and its internal source, something quite unusual occurred. It surprised even me, although I had been the one developing and supervising the method. This was truly different: three weeks after the event, the Ministry announced it had *officially* selected the values of the entire organization! Henceforth, all decisions made were to be based on the criteria of adherence to said values. The values? Five of the six values produced through the direct input of the employee populace!

Soon afterward, posters with the new values were sprouting up in our offices everywhere, and the Better Together initiative became on-going with a booklet and intranet mechanism for ongoing employee feedback and input.

One year later the Alberta Public Service, with over 32,000 employees announced that they too had developed a Values initiative. Their values? Four of the five developed through my work at the Ministry of Restructuring and Government Efficiency.

What is the role of emotion vs. logic in branding?

In 1971, a retail coffee bean outlet opened in Seattle. This single store created a local reputation for quality and ran fairly much this way until 1983. At that time Howard Schultz joined the company and, after a visit to Italy, had the idea that store should create a gathering place selling espresso and ready-brewed coffee as he had seen abroad. After the shareholders rejected his idea, Schultz went off and opened his own business, *Il Giornale*, which was fairly successful. He opened a couple of locations and people started to line up for the experience. In 1987, Shultz had the opportunity to acquire the original coffee bean outlet, and combined the brands, allowing him to create his original vision. The result was Starbucks, very much as we know it today. When Starbucks went public in 1995, it had 165 outlets.

Bypassing the brain—creating market leverage beyond the level of reason is the ultimate goal of every brand. By appealing to the unconscious, a brand can develop a level of magnetic pull and attraction that dramatically alters the business model—creating efficiencies and developing loyalties with a reach well beyond the capacity of any singular human effort. This also allows effective new or emerging brands to spring forward rapidly—literally leveraged beyond reason.

By creating a brand around the concept of popularity itself, Howard Schultz hit on a "gestalt" or pattern of the moment that accurately tapped into an area where Westerners were facing an emotional gap. Our ideas of family and home were disintegrating rapidly but the fundamental need to be seen with others—to belong—be part of an inclusive popular group, were as strong as ever. Starbucks provides this through brand identification to a pre-existing popular archetype—that of the ever-popular (but hard to access) virgin.

Language, including use of form and color, is instrumental in unconscious identification. In the case of Starbucks, (which conforms to the Tower archetype—think Rapunzel of story book fame) the prevalent use of (virginal) spring green, the circular (female) logo and even the mermaid motif (again, virgin) in the logo on every cup all reinforce the ideal of the virgin.

Webster defines identification as a mental mechanism wherein the individual gains gratification, emotional support, or relief from anxiety by attributing to himself consciously or unconsciously the characteristics of another person or group; or orientation of the self in regard to something with a resulting feeling of close emotional association.

With respect to brands, therefore, identification occurs when an individual gains gratification, emotional support or relief from anxiety through a brand experience or orients him/herself to it with a feeling of strong emotional association or preference for a brand over all competing entities. Individuals who identify with a brand are not easily swayed from their choice. People choose emotionally (based on gut feeling or instinct) and then justify their decisions rationally.

Weak or poor brand identification is extremely costly to an organization because rationality in human beings does not always dominate; therefore, reason may easily be subverted by powerful emotional identification from a competing brand. The heart, gut and libido together pull more strongly than the brain! An individual with strong identification to a brand makes purchasing decisions based on "gut feeling", or any number of other reasons he or she may come up with (including logical ones developed after the fact), to justify their preference.

For every emotional requirement we can derive a psychological domain, or reference area. Each area relates to a fundamental question we all ask. For instance, the primal requirement for sexual attractiveness relates to the psychological domain of popularity. This is the case for Starbucks' (as in all brands of the Tower type). The question relating to the domain of popularity is "Who?" A typical promise is You, Only Better. In this manner, brands such as Starbucks deliver an emotionally satisfying response to prevailing gaps in the human condition.

Starbucks, and other brands including government departments, initiatives and even not-for-profits, can possess market leverage beyond reason because they successfully deliver an appropriate brand proposition to an existing market need tied to unconscious metaphors that are congruent with their brand positioning.

Tim Hortons vs: Starbucks

March 2015. With four hours of sleep and a workshop to show up for at 6:50 a.m. I needed coffee! Was I thinking change? No. This time I was just thinking caffeine. But, I was also thinking of impressions. And convenience. There is an independent coffee shop I had in mind, but there's a Starbucks in the grocery store on the way. Starbucks it is!

Walking in with a couple minutes to spare, I thought briefly about my order. Usually a 'tall' Americano 'with room'. However, I felt like I wanted something a little different, and little taller than a tall (small in non-Starbucksese). I ordered a 'grande' cappuccino and chatted with the 'barista' as she made my beverage. Green mermaid-emblazoned white cup in-hand I left the store, tucking the cup neatly into the cup-holder of our Mercedes-Benz. So comfortable, so appropriate, so 'right'.

Starbucks is a Tower Brand. Other competitors in this space include The Body Shop (British cosmetics firm) and Barbie (American doll of sex-kitten proportions made by Mattel).

In the space of quick serve there are few competitors using the Tower Brand category, one of many reasons that Starbucks was able to enter a saturated marketplace and soak up so much business that no one else saw. In a world of Dunkin' Donuts and 49c drip coffee who needs $3 coffee you have to stand and wait for?

A lot of people, it turns out!

In Canada Starbucks' strongest rival is Tim Horton's. This Canadian-made brand (now owned by a Brazillian-controlled conglomerate which also controls Burger King) named after a Canadian hockey hero was once the only game in town.

A typical 'house brand' 'Tim's', as it is affectionately known by millions of Canadians is a drive-through staple for thousands of commuters every morning looking for the 'double-double' (Canadian for two creams, two sugars). At Tim Horton's, unlike at Starbucks, there is no barista, and you don't doctor your own coffee. You order from the counter (or drive-through) the way you want it, and it is served to you a few moments later in a brown cup with a bright red friendly script logo. The price? About one-half of Starbucks higher priced brew.

Unspoken promises create strong loyalties.

"Let's meet for coffee!" has now become a dividing line for Canadians. The response, *Tim's* or *Starbucks* divides along cultural, class and philosophical lines. And the opinions (from normally mild-mannered, polite Canadians) are telling.

"I don't like Starbucks coffee, it tastes burnt," is one refrain.

"Let's meet at Starbucks," is another (as if there is no alternative).

Why the antipathy?

Is this a war between coffee flavors? Not really.

This is a battle between philosophies.

The archetypal inhabitant of all Tower brands (communicating in Green or Pink is the tip-off) is the Virgin. In contrast, the owner of the House brand (Tim's communicates using red and yellow) is the Whore!

These two 'daughters' of the Palace brand 'mother' could not possibly have two more different characters. They are both representative of popular 'mean' girls in junior high, but from two very different camps. One, the stuck-up Virgin, who runs the popular group and the other, easier girl, who is popular for different reasons. One you're proud to run with. The other, well, you're happy you know her too.

For differing emotional reasons (and sometimes at different times) these archetypes both have a strong pull. In image-conscious urban markets where being part of the 'in-group' is de rigueur and hipster style outweighs budgetary constraints, the Tower brand has greater appeal. And in small-town, suburban and commuter worlds where convenience is a trump card, the House brand mixture of comfort and 'come as you are' attitude with 'down-home' pricing and service wins.

There would be no point in these two rivals directly competing on price or product. The irrational, emotional pull is on such a different register that it is unlikely one could ever put the other out of business.

But do we smell fear? Recently Tim Horton's started offering upmarket Cappucino's and 'lattes'. And suddenly they have two blends of drip coffee, regular and 'dark'. What's going on here?

Too soon to say about success, but I suspect that there's a social component here for Canadians. The battle line isn't about where 'I' will go for coffee, it's where 'We' will go. Are Tim Horton's new beverages a tip of the hat to Canadians who can't agree on a coffee shop to meet at?

I think that's exactly what Tim Horton's is doing and I will be interested to see what the results are.

Unlike Coca-Cola's (Palace Brand) response to Pepsi's (Hotel Brand) challenge of the late 70s, Tim's House Brand strategy does not conflict with the brand's archetype. The unasked question of House brands is "What?", not 'When?'. And the promise of 'more for less' does not conflict with adding flavors similar to that of rivals and charging less. In fact, this is exactly the philosophy and strategy of a successful house brand!

Congratulations to Tim Horton's on its introduction of a darker, Starbucks-like flavor, to its mix, while not changing, and continuing to offer its medium-brewed, familiar flavor alongside.

Learning to understand and play with archetypal brand formulas is important to maintaining nimble tactics in an ever-changing competitive landscape, but having a deep understanding (and sticking with) your brand strategy is vital. Strategy, once chosen, should never change, while tactics may evolve frequently.

The first time I saw a Starbucks was in the 90s when the company first expanded across the USA Canadian border into Vancouver. Within two years, the company had opened two locations on the same intersection on popular Robson Street (on opposite sides of the street). Why? Because there was too much volume at the first store (you couldn't enter for the line-ups). What was going on?

Howard Shultz purchased Starbucks, at the time a coffee bean roaster in the Pike Street Market, in the late 70s and developed a vision of providing an 'Italian-style' coffee bar in America. With a background in packaged products, Shultz knew and understood packaging, branding and American tastes. Yes, he took a chance with his 'Italian-style' concept and had to make some significant tweaks at first before he hit on the winning formula. But boy, did he get lucky with his persistence!

The famous Starbucks mermaid is an almost perfect representation of every aspect of the Tower Brand. The original logo and name were aspects that Shultz purchased with the company. The rest was his. The Italian names for coffees, and unique sizes, the idea of 'baristas' who operate the shiny and ornate espresso machine. The homey, inviting décor and style of service were also innovations.

Coke & Apple

Did you know that both Apple computer and Coca-Cola soda run on essentially the same brand formula? They are both Palace Brands.

That means they both communicate an unspoken promise in response to an 'unasked question'. This question; the question that always comes with Palace Brands, is 'when?"

The answer, for both Apple and Coca-Cola is the same in essence, because they both play the Palace brand game, just like Toyota and Rolls-Royce. The answer: always. The promise: forever, that is (ultimately) immortality!

These are big promises.

Brands work on archetypal pathways, like characters in a book or a play. Unlike in books, however, there is a very limited number of successful (proven) archetypes for brands. So, oftentimes, what appear to be quite dissimilar companies or brands actually overlap quite generally in their process and outcome.

Let's take a look: Both Coke and Apple have been number one in Interbrand's annual rating of the top 100 brands. Recently, Apple has overtaken Coke and displaced it as the number one most valuable global brand.

Both brands operate on the female archetype of the matriarch whose ultimate promise is timelessness. It's 'always Coca-Cola', and 'forever Coke'. In like manner, Apple has positioned itself as the timeless technology company that everyone else must catch up with. Design and advertising in both cases plays a key role in the establishment and continuity of this positioning. Timeless, classic designs are their keynotes and underscore their marketing campaigns; even while seasonally updated, they play against a standard backdrop: The darkened stage for Apple events, timeless icons, like Santa Claus, for Coca-Cola.

In numerous other ways both brands conform to the archetype of the eternal Mother whose strong presence and care serve to dispel both non-believers and doubt from the converted. This excellent recipe is played out time and again for brands of this type (other brands using this type include Rolls Royce, Toyota and Xerox, but nowhere has it been as well demonstrated, both in success and in failure than with Coca-Cola, and Apple.

The Coke/Apple formula, or generically the Palace Brand Archetype, as we refer to it, is not the only super successful formula out there. What about Google, Amazon and Facebook? Each of these internet startups has unwittingly hit upon already proven formulae that work equally well in traditional firms—they simply moved faster due to their digital medium being one with the times.

Companies that at first appear to be unrelated are frequently competitors for the same emotions. Look beyond the obvious of product category to the unspoken promise of a brand to understand who it is truly talking to, and what it is saying, as well as where it is reaching to.

Naïve: True Branding Stories

Do you compete in category, or promise?

Friendly Technology Corp., started by my parents, notably my mother, was aiming to deliver a promise of 'hand-holding' and ease of use to computer buyers, most of whom were novices, at the time. In the 1980s, most new computer buyers were brand new, they had never before owned, or operated a computer. This meant there was quite a bit of 'hand holding', training and support involved. Friendly Tech was well positioned to provide buyers with the support and service—as well as the computers they required. Mother was fantastic on the phone with people supporting long technical questions she had no direct answer to, yet pursued nevertheless, to solution with her patient, methodical, intelligent, inquiring way. In person, in the store she was graceful and efficient in her stylish way of organizing things, and possibly a little charming as well. I learned quickly it was vital I find what these business clients wanted to do with a computer so that I could find a way

One day, however, we got some news that would forever change our business. Three blocks away, a large and successful local drugstore chain (London Drugs) had added a computer department. Obviously, I was very interested to investigate. Sure enough, in a room tucked away behind the paper towels, toaster ovens and film developing department, was a small new area packed to the rafters with boxes of computers, selling for extremely low prices. To add to the dilemma, everything was illustrated in a mass circular flyer distributed to hundreds of thousands of households. I had nowhere near the budget to compete with either the advertising or the stock levels.

Obviously, the service at London Drugs was not the same as that at our store, but that, for the moment was not my chief concern: we were losing business to a drug store! What to do? Our director suggested we erect a prominent billboard that said 'We don't sell Aspirin'. While a cute idea, this did not really land. The trouble was many new customers were no longer persuaded by our superior service. And, with our 'boutique' volume, we just could not compete on prices of the big chain drugstore, which was buying volumes far in excess of our single outlet store.

Customers were becoming increasingly savvy, meaning they shopped around and most got wind of the cheap computer prices at the local drug store. Now, when they came into our store they wanted to know if we could 'match prices'. Selling our (bundled in) hand-holding support and bend-over-backwards service up front to neophyte users was difficult when they frequently did not realize until after their purchase how much assistance would be required. This was years before computers became as reliable, easy or commonplace as they are today. Customers simply saw a price tag 15-20 percent lower on a large ticket item (This was close to our entire profit margin). It did not help that at that time even basic computers cost well over $1,000 (this was with two floppy drives—no hard disk, and a basic monochrome screen).

Category or Promise? Author Insight

So, were we competing in the category of computer stores, or was something else happening? At the time I was years from formulating the contents of this book. But, it was easy to see, even at the time that the PROMISE of cheap prices outweighed the CATEGORY expertise of being a specialized computer store.

What did we do? Like many others before us, we specialized. We decided to focus on the area of our business with the greatest amount of knowledge and service and specialized products the drugstore did not yet carry. For a time, this worked, but it soon became a matter of staying 'one step ahead', for sure enough wherever we went, London Drugs seemed to follow a season later!

Unfortunately for Friendly Technology, this strategy; while it kept our doors open, did not accumulate much profit, and like many small business owners, after half a dozen years of this we could no longer keep up the effort. It was too much work for too little reward. We closed shop and went our ways.

In this way, my first Marketing job was both a failure, and a success. I failed to expand the business. I succeeded in determining two things, at least to myself:

1. There had to be 'a better way', and
2. There was clearly 'something missing', which I was determined to find out about, and learn, then master!

My intent is to help you become a brand insider, learning to see brands as a strategist acting through color, form, and language to create desire, guiding the design of websites, books, brochures, games, merchandising and employee engagement programs that work on an almost magical level to produce participative behavior that is predictable, profitable and prescient in nature.

Naïve?

"Did you know that Evian spelled backwards is Naïve?" my friend Justin was sipping from a bottle of water as I drove the twisty highway up to neighboring Flagstaff.

"Did you know you can see that by looking through the new transparent bottle design from the back?" I responded.

Sometimes a secret, needs to be let out of a bag.

Evian is a premium bottled water from Évian-les-Bains in France, which sells for up to six or eight times the price of other bottled waters. Selling in the same red, white and blue brand space of Pepsi and Red Bull, how can a water deliver on the same promise as a caffeinated beverage. What is the unspoken promise?

Hotel brands, like Evian respond to the question "Which Way?" with the answer 'Your way' and a promise of change or choice, ultimately delivering on an experience of transformation.

What if I want to be renewed? One way is the 80s rebellious 'choice of a new generation', another is 'getting wings' Red Bull-style. Evian's is by returning us to our roots. Naïve is literally to remove the worldly grime, exposure and cynicism of the day to day world, returning to a child-like innocent state of cleanliness and purity. Look again at the tactical exploitation of the Hotel strategy contrasting most distinctly between Pepsi's strong saturated graphical design and colors with Evian's subtle, pastel execution of the same basic design brief which might be described as 'use red white (or silver) and blue with a 'contrasting' design that is both masculine and feminine in nature'.

In this way the same brand archetype may be used to address quite differing market areas and demographics (or times of day and desires). At the same time, a singular customer psychology can be said to be at play in either situation, with little need to compete with the other.

In the late 70s when Pepsi came out with its blind taste test challenge, media attention was temporarily drawn to the nature of the fight. The idea of underdog Pepsi 'coming out fighting' and directly stating they were

better than Coke was 'taking the gloves off' in the marketing world of that day. At that time (and still today) it was relatively rare for a brand to directly mention a competitor brand in their advertising. After all, there is a risk you may end up inadvertently promoting your competitor. It is a risky, ballsy tactic. It worked.

In fact, I am pretty sure it worked better than anyone at Pepsi could have dreamed of.

What happened next has been written about so many times, and is the subject of so many marketing theses I'll try to keep my description short and to the point.

Coke blinked.

Coke forgot (corporate memories are notoriously short) that it wasn't in the Cola business. Coca-Cola is in the Forever business. But Pepsi's ballsy, in-your-face marketing campaign had hit Coke where it hurt the most—their pride. Insinuating that Pepsi's sweeter beverage was, in fact, preferable to Coke was so effective that the powers at Coke actually believed it was true.

In April 1985 Coke announced it was changing it's formula. Henceforth the beverage would be known as 'New Coke' and the product had a new lighter, yet somehow sweeter taste.

Customer reaction was swift and violent.

Never before in marketing history has a consumer brand had such a large-scale, vitriolic, angry reaction from customers. Customers recoiled at grocery stores where the new product was displayed. Shipments of 'old Coke' were hoarded and auctioned to the highest bidder. Angry letters to the editor were written. Coke had screwed up and they knew it.

Within 30 days Coca-Cola reintroduced the original Coke, alongside new Coke with the moniker "Coca-Cola Classic". For over twenty years {?}, to save face, Coke had to double its production facilities making two differing versions of the product, causing endless customer confusion and returns at the store, and hundreds of millions in advertising to straighten out the perceptual mess. In typical fashion big name celebrities were brought in to pitch the new product, and then the return of the old. Talk about inefficiency! Coke competing with Coke and Pepsi laughing all the way to the bank.

Today New Coke is nowhere to be found and, at long last the word 'Classic' has finally been dropped from Coke's packaging. Today's Coca-Cola? Almost identical package to that seen before 1979.

Where did Coca-Cola screw up?

1. Thought they were competing in product category, not unspoken promise territory.
2. Forgot their own unspoken promise and developed a marketing tactic flying directly in the face of it.

Think of it: how can 'forever' be 'new'? Brand tactics (marketing, or any that refer to resource allocation) MUST be in alignment with brand strategy, which is directly informed by an examination of brand archetype.

When consumers heard and saw Coke's 1979 strategy two opposing things presented themselves in direct misalignment. 1.) and unconscious, emotional, intuitive 'truth' (Coke is forever) and 2.) a conscious, rational, logical 'truth' (Coke has changed, Coke is new). These two concepts do not sit well with each other. One must be false. So, which is (or was) false?

Was Coke forever, or was Coke new?

Facing this dilemma, the intuitive truth will almost always win out. People buy emotionally and justify rationally. Combined with a (somewhat) addictive substance (both sugar and caffeine may have addictive qualities) the typical consumer broke into a cold sweat!

What the hell was Coke up to?

To paraphrase another catchphrase from a few years later "I want my Coke," was the swift reaction, and this was so forcefully delivered that is actually what consumers got. New Coke was withdrawn from the market.

Red Bull gives you winnnnnnnngs!

"Come on, Bryce!" my friend Justin is trying to convince me to go out.

"I have a 6:50 workshop in the morning…" I may be fooling him, but I'm not fooling myself. I *do* want to go out. I *want* to drive the hour up to Flagstaff, the nearest town with a nightclub. I *want* to be free, not give a damn and pay the consequences tomorrow!

But now that I'm here, at the nightclub, staring the pretty bartender in the face, and deciding what to order, I do know one thing—alcohol is not my friend, right now. It's one thing to face an all-day workshop with on four hours of sleep (inevitable at this stage), it's quite another to do so while feeling hung-over!

"Two Red Bulls," I order.

"Anything else?"

"Two glasses of water."

The familiar artwork on the small can fills my hand comfortable as I make my way through the crowded drag show audience back to Justin. He's happy. He thinks he convinced me to come out with him tonight. Well. I *let* him convince me.

Right now, I'm enjoying the moment, knowing the combined jolt of stimulants and carbonated sugar water are working their magic.

Red Bull took advantage of a gap in the 'energy drink' market, leaving moribund by Pepsi/Coke, which for two long have focused on their chief rivals as the only game in town; behind. Coming from behind, Red Bull invented a new format (smaller packaging) with focused intention (concentrated buzz) and modern sensibilities (less sweet) specifically directed to a trend-setting audience (the night club demographic).

What's so interesting is that this market take-over was so 'sleeper' that Coke and Pepsi don't seem to have even noticed. Possibly the volume numbers are so small, relative to their overall market share it doesn't seem to matter to them. But Red Bull's strategy is precisely aimed for Pepsi's demographic *and*, more importantly, Pepsi's brand archetype. Red Bull is a wedge.

Are Pepsi and Coke competitors? How to usurp an elephant (one bottled beverage at a time).

Previously we discussed both the Pepsi Challenge, and the Red Bull slogan and co-opted night club distribution strategy. Is it possible these are both excellent tactics for their times? Let's take a look.

Today's cola war is subtler. For one thing the entire beverage industry has shifted and got mixed up. beginning in 2000 water overtook colas as a beverage category. Colas in general have been declining as percentage of the mix for years. People just aren't that interested or motivated by flavor categories any longer. Benefit categories (energy drinks, health drinks, vitamin drinks, sports drinks) are the new rage.

What do you do when your category is being usurped?

Get back to basics!

(Re-)Examine your unspoken promise. Dig into your archetype!

What does Pepsi stand for? Change!

What are Pepsi customers really buying? Transformation!

Who else is selling this? Red Bull!

In brands, as in human relationships, it pays to look beyond the obvious. People say one thing and do another. Examining inner motives, unspoken questions and unstated promises fills out the dynamic, charting new ways to examine our competitive landscape by completing a 'dreamscape' that while hidden, is all the more powerful for being unstated, all the stronger for being almost totally unconscious.

Both Pepsi and Red Bull communicate on the 'red, white and blue' pathway that we call the Hotel archetype. As we have discussed, the Hotel returns an unstated promise of transformation to the unasked question 'Which way?'. I have a choice! Stay home, be responsible, have an early night, or go out?

"Stay home," a small, boring, logical voice inside me said.

"Get going!" yelled my intuitive right brain. I got going.

Now, Red Bull in hand, feeling the gentle warmth of energy flooding my body and mind, Red Bull's catch phrase "Red Bull gives you winnnnngs!" comes to mind. It's exactly what I needed and wanted at that moment. I am transformed, and that was the choice I wanted after having asked myself the Hotel brand question "Which way?" just one hour earlier.

Pepsi, like Red Bull, communicates the same overall meta-message, but with a somewhat different story, package, product and at a much lower

price point. Ounce for ounce Red Bull must be about five or six times the price of Pepsi, but here I am, Red Bull in hand—not a Pepsi in sight.

Illustrated at left: Chinese Pepsi "ENERGY COLA": As a Hotel Brand Pepsi is free to vary it's formula and offerings. Note Red Bull-style cans.

Let's look at three differing stories emerging from very similar products:

Brand	Coke	Pepsi	Red Bull
Brand archetype	Palace	Hotel	Hotel
Communicates on (color channel)	Red	Red, white & blue	Red, white and blue
Unspoken promise	Forever	Change, transformation	Change, transformation
Historic Slogan	Always Coca-Cola	The Choice of a New Generation	Red Bull gives you winnnngs!
Standard serving format (can size)	24 carton 12 fl oz cans	18 carton 12 fl oz Cans	24 carton 8.4 fl oz cans
Usual retail price (Walmart)	$9.00 $.04/fl oz	$10.99 $.06/fl oz	$35.68 $.18/fl oz
Leading distribution point	Fast food restaurants, McDonald's	Fast food, KFC, Taco Bell	Independent night clubs
Slogan	TASTE THE FEELING®	CHILL POP FUN®	WINGS WHEN YOU NEED THEM®

In the chart above you see: the original, the wannabe, and what's happening. For instance, would people say "Pepsi is the choice of a new generation," when they grab a can and join their friends? Or would they yell "Red Bull gives you winnnngs!"? I'm not sure they're saying either, but I'm feel if it was, it would likely be the latter. Red Bull's slogan is in vernacular of the moment, and in a party moment I can see it happening. Pepsi's boardroom approved style is way too staid for today's counter culture. And fountain drinks? So old.

Curiously, both Coke and Pepsi have started to distribute in a new, smaller can format. But Red Bull, coming stealthily from behind, has already stolen the show. What we can say is that the territory packaged sweet carbonated beverages with an unspoken promise of change has been usurped by Red Bull. Pepsi is no longer the only (hotel brand carbonated beverage) game in town.

When it comes to competition, the one constant you can rely on is change.

That is why it pays to get deep into your brand, helping it feel more and more satisfying by connecting closer and closer with more and more people. One of the best ways is discussed next.

BRAND IDENTIFICATION:

PERSEUS
Personally Emotive Reciprocal Spirit Express Universal Solution

Movement is the primary physical communicator of brand messaging. Movement has the potential to grab and hold attention, creating brand personality.

D4 MarkBrand Creative has developed Personally Emotive Reciprocal Spirit Express Universal Solution (PERSEUS), a methodology including partner engagement through specific training curriculum, which engages on a personal level and brings brand messaging to the level of inspiration.

Architectonics helps us understand which archetypal metaphors relate most closely to universal messages expressed on a human level.

PERSEUS shares a living message for brands.

The Media Lab of Live Events

Detailed planning and many levels and kinds of design work go into Live Events.

For one event alone, like this illustrated, there was concept, strategy, graphic design, room layout, surveying, plastics, manufacturing, coordinating with trades, lighting, costuming, hair, makeup, photography, video, coordination and talent!

At left, professional dancers in the center of the Canadian Iceberg Vodka Action Bar designed for Fashion Cares at the Metro Toronto Convention Center, Canada.

Below: elevation plans.

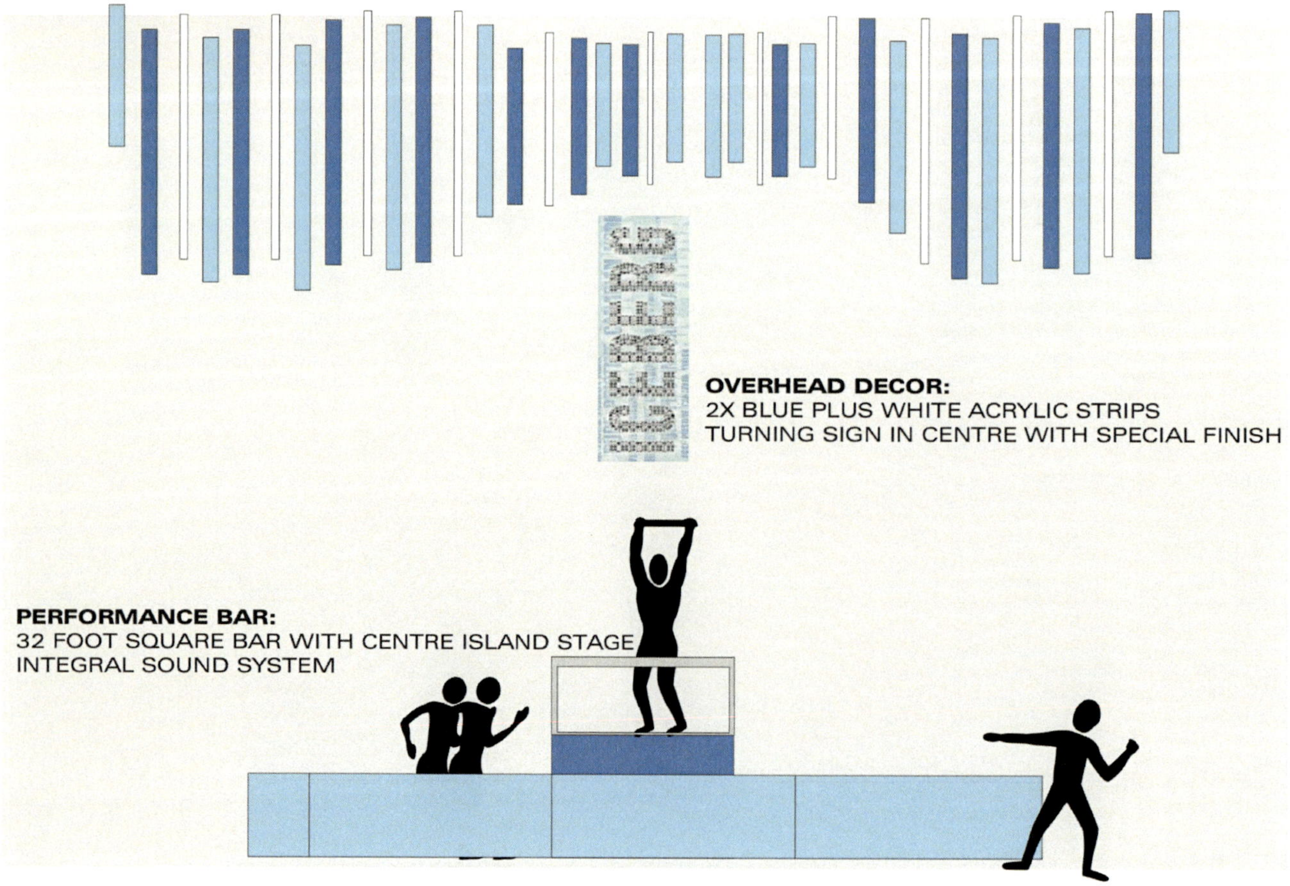

OVERHEAD DECOR:
2X BLUE PLUS WHITE ACRYLIC STRIPS
TURNING SIGN IN CENTRE WITH SPECIAL FINISH

PERFORMANCE BAR:
32 FOOT SQUARE BAR WITH CENTRE ISLAND STAGE
INTEGRAL SOUND SYSTEM

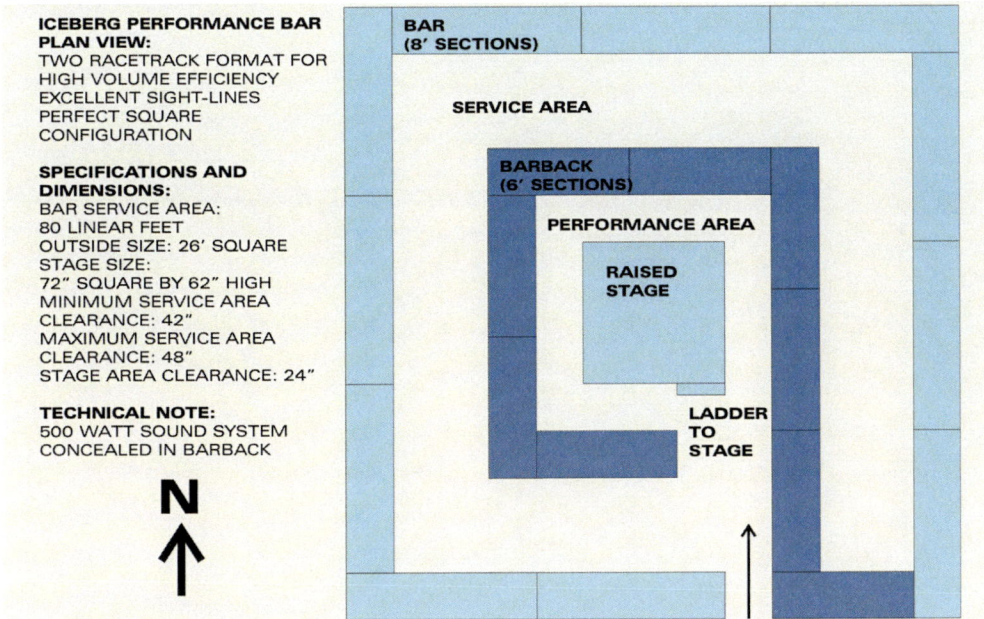

**ICEBERG PERFORMANCE BAR
PLAN VIEW:**
TWO RACETRACK FORMAT FOR
HIGH VOLUME EFFICIENCY
EXCELLENT SIGHT-LINES
PERFECT SQUARE
CONFIGURATION

**SPECIFICATIONS AND
DIMENSIONS:**
BAR SERVICE AREA:
80 LINEAR FEET
OUTSIDE SIZE: 26' SQUARE
STAGE SIZE:
72" SQUARE BY 62" HIGH
MINIMUM SERVICE AREA
CLEARANCE: 42"
MAXIMUM SERVICE AREA
CLEARANCE: 48"
STAGE AREA CLEARANCE: 24"

TECHNICAL NOTE:
500 WATT SOUND SYSTEM
CONCEALED IN BARBACK

N

**BAR
(8' SECTIONS)**

SERVICE AREA

**BARBACK
(6' SECTIONS)**

PERFORMANCE AREA

**RAISED
STAGE**

**LADDER
TO
STAGE**

*This bar was designed to deliver drinks and brand spectacle to 8,000 guests (plan
view above, photograph, below)*

EVENT BRAND:
ICEBERG
PURE PRISTINE CANADIAN VODKA

MOTIF DESIGN:
CASINO MOTIF HAND-MADE TYPE
EXECUTED IN SPECIAL FINISH
DESIGN IS COHERENT WITH OVERALL EVENT

Detailed scale drawing and design schematic for special logo treatment (above).

I feel that events are still being underutilized. I want to underscore their value in brand building, when properly planned. Part of the reason events are still underutilized is lack of holistic design, which denies them their full

efficiency potential. Being 'all-in' makes a difference.

An 'event' can technically be any kind of pre-arranged multi-person meeting. There is hardly a better way to garner attention, shift polarities and create change than through live events. Did I mention they're also fun?

Media Lab

I like the concept of a 'media lab' to drive home the value of the authenticity and energy that only a live event can achieve.

Given that marketing; branding, and sales are inexact sciences it makes sense to be constantly monitoring and correcting these activities. There is no faster to get the instant feedback at a profit than by live events run as a media lab.

Rather than developing a single regional, national or global campaign, through the media lab of live events, a brand can take the wisdom of the startup world to iteratively launch major products, finding out in advance which features to highlight, and which not to, for instance.

The launch of the future may be an evolving network series of events that feedback data for the next activities, and events, and the next, creating a whirling dervish of positive feedback. With appropriate mechanisms it could even be possible to develop products this way, with widespread inputs to their design, circuitry, image and purpose.

Live Events Promote Brand Identification

Original illustration by Eddee, commissioned ca 2001 by the Author for postcard.

With the energy that creates worlds behind them, live events sound great, but to be a true media opportunity for Brand Identification, the criteria are specific and include the following:

- Works on many individuals (hundreds or thousands) at once
- Develops heightened emotion in at in a congruent way with brand
- Does not depend on any one individual or charismatic presentation
- Solves through Brand Identification an Emotional Gap via communication of the Unspoken Promise.

Solving these criteria without prolonged expenditure of millions of dollars is made possible by first monopolizing context, and then focusing attention. Monopolizing context is necessary first, because our society exposes individuals to literally thousands of brand messages per day. In order to develop emotional resonance, we must first remove most of this competition and then get the individual in a receptive emotional state. Focusing attention is required because Brand Identification is a process which requires both rational and emotional engagement to produce the desired effect, which includes both a purchasing decision and loyalty (i.e. residual purchasing decisions).

As we will see, no other single media offers the full spectrum of developing an Emotional Gap compared to a Customer (i.e. Sponsored) Event. Events are the most effective method to monopolize context. Within this context virtually every aspect of personal environment can be controlled thereby permitting the development of any set of desirable circumstances, which may be designed to produce any predictable emotional outcome within a given audience.

Let's look at thirteen means and methods available within a Live Event to develop Emotional Gap, while touching on other media for comparison:

Mean	Method	How It Works	Available in Other Media?
Olfactory	Food preparation and service delivery, foliage, flowers, candles, perfumes, etc.	The sense of smell is one of the strongest of all emotional registers	Scratch & Sniff, i.e. Magazine or direct-mail samples, Perfumed Environments or packaging.

Visual	Venue selection, Controlled (theatrical) Lighting, Projections of any size, Draping, Set Pieces including Furnishings, Decor, Floral and Foliage, Human Props (extras), Costumes, Product Placement, Presentations, etc.	Seeing is believing	Retail is the only other medium offering direct inspection; magazines offer high quality still image reproduction in small formats; large-screen HDTV is the closest simulation. Augmented Reality interrupts Visual in an interesting way. Virtual Reality is developing.
Auditory / Acoustic	Live and Pre-recorded Music, Public Announcements, Human Props, Product Demonstrations, etc.	Many individuals need to hear a message before it registers	Widely available: i.e. Internet, radio, TV; main limitation with other media is reproduction quality and volume is not controlled—may have undesired interference from other sources
Kinesthetic / Touch	Human Touch, Product Sample, Set Pieces (i.e. velvet drapery), etc.	Some individuals need to touch or be touched before they'll buy	Retail is currently the only other medium offering direct touch and the warmth of human contact, as well as the opportunity to "touch it"

Taste	Food and Beverage Service	Few activities offer the primacy of eating in developing an emotional bond	Other media offering taste include grocery store sampling and direct-mail sample offers as well as 'going for lunch'.
Saltation	Rhythmic Movement may be delivered through Dance, Animatronic Displays, Moving Lights (such as strobe or mirror-ball effects), etc.	Saltation is a key ingredient in the Brand Identification process; producing an hypnotic effect conducive to an emotionally receptive state	Television is the main medium which sometimes employs this technique, Animated Window Displays may also use rhythmic movement to intense effect
Linear Movement	Event design may develop a controlled pathway or circuit which individuals traverse from beginning to end	Linear Movement allows successive layers of emotional resonance and information delivery in a predictable order	Radio and television offer a simulation of linear movement—however neither actually requires personal movement—therefore interaction (and emotional engagement) is limited. Magazines offer a simulation—but flipping is too easy. Retail may offer this (think Ikea)

Sensory Overload	Controlled Lighting, Sound, and all prior mentioned methods may be combined in a controlled manner	Sensory Overload may briefly overstimulate the nervous system producing a "high" or euphoria conducive to receptivity	Retail may produce sensory overload—the challenge within this medium is limiting the duration of the overload. Due to the uncontrolled timeframe this is a difficulty which has not been systematically addressed yet. Television aims for this but the remote control returns control to the individual
Sensory Deprivation	Darkness, full draping, muffled sounds or obscured views	Creates a need to move forward—develops an emotional gap which must be filled	No other media besides possibly VR offers the emotional resonance of this theatrical method
Product Demonstration	Group presentations, PowerPoints, Film & Video and Hands-On demonstrations	Invites individuals to learn more, experience best-case scenarios as well as real-world testing	Depending on the product, this method may be explored through many types of media including internet, radio, TV, magazines and even direct-mail. The best live demonstrations are offered through retail,

			and so are the worst
Product Sampling	May involve kiosks, person-to-person interaction, role-play, table games or other interactivities	One-on-one trial of specific features or customizations	Very limited in other media, but depending on the product, offered by Direct Mail, Magazine Insert and Retail
Group Dynamics (Peer Influence)	Crowd dynamics developed through presentation, audience participation, video display feedback systems, etc.	Many individuals who will not initiate movement without peer approval will gladly do so when they see others act	The combination of media developed in effective traditional campaigns produces this effect, as do Telethons and other instant feedback system such as many on-line social media systems
Product Exposition & Purchasing Opportunities	On-site registration, forms completion, sit-down or stand-up kiosks, mini-mall, retail venue set-up	After being influenced by twelve prior means a strong Emotional Gap is developed which for many will be filled with an on-the-spot commitment to purchase	Retail offers the most proven and satisfying experience to most. Television, combined with call-center, internet with e-commerce and magazine with mail-order offer Product Exposition & Purchasing Opportunities. No other media exceeds a

Customer Event at developing an Emotional Gap and then fulfilling it through Brand Identification

There is an extremely wide range of media choices available through the marketplace, but most work best in serial conjunction with others and are dependent on a retail presence; therefore, requiring relatively vast expenditure on an on-going basis to produce brand identification.

Because they both monopolize context and focus attention, Customer Events offer an effective stand-alone media alternative in fulfilling Marketing goals. With thirteen or more means available, Customer Events offer the immediacy, emotional resonance and direction that Brands need to develop Brand Identification with individuals rapidly, deeply, and well at a predictable cost.

Now that you understand the vital importance of connecting emotionally with customers, and how, through the Unspoken Promise, you do so, I hope that you are beginning to see strategic opportunities in a few of these areas:

- Pricing
- Growth
- Licensing
- Advertising
- Relationships
- Staffing
- Sales

If you are interested in applying these tactics, including the spotlight generated by events, the next section will interest you: *Scents of Success*.

CRONOS

Chronological Reciprocal Organized Nominal Ordered System

D4
MarkBrand
CREATIVE

Order is the final communicator of brand messaging

D4 MarkBrand Creative has developed Chronological Reciprocal Organized Nominal Ordered Standard (CRONOS), a system which builds reciprocal relatedness with all branding stakeholders over time.

Architectonics helps us understand what roles and which individuals resonate most closely to specifically ordered development areas.

CRONOS joins named entities in measurable areas of development and success over time.

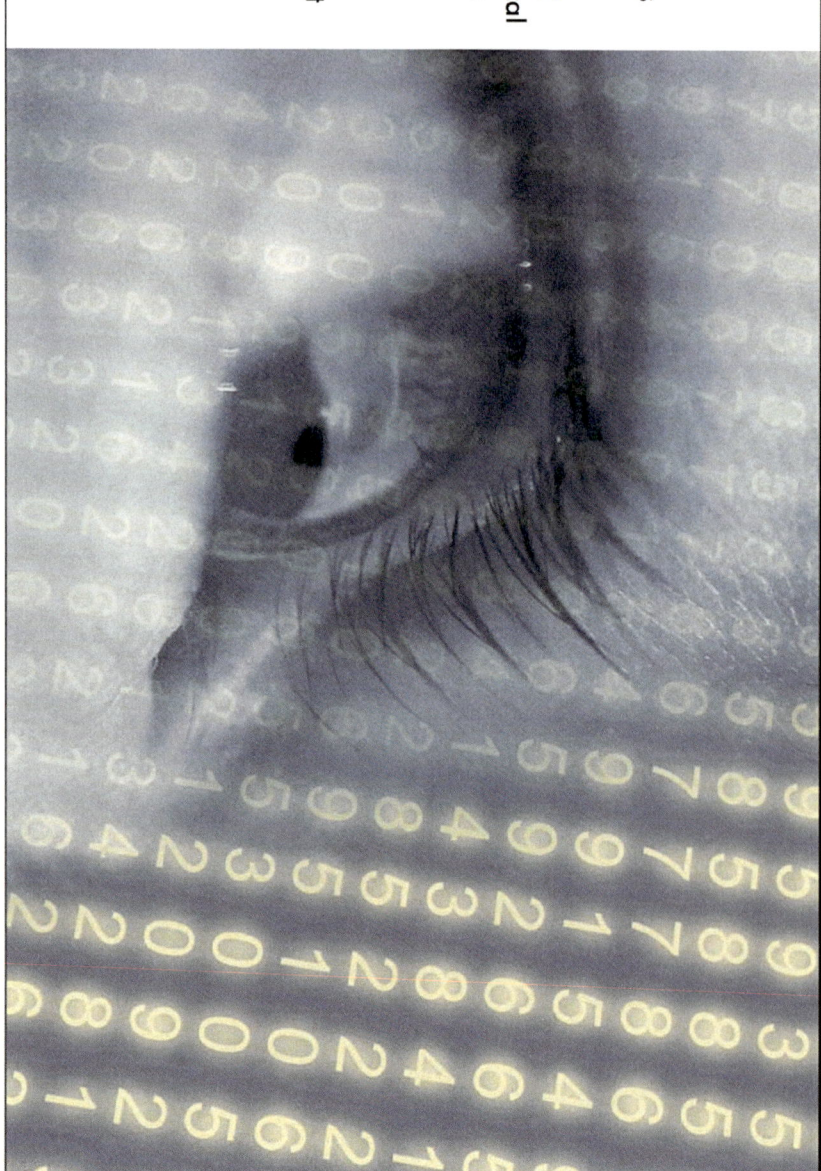

4

VALUATION

SUCCESS

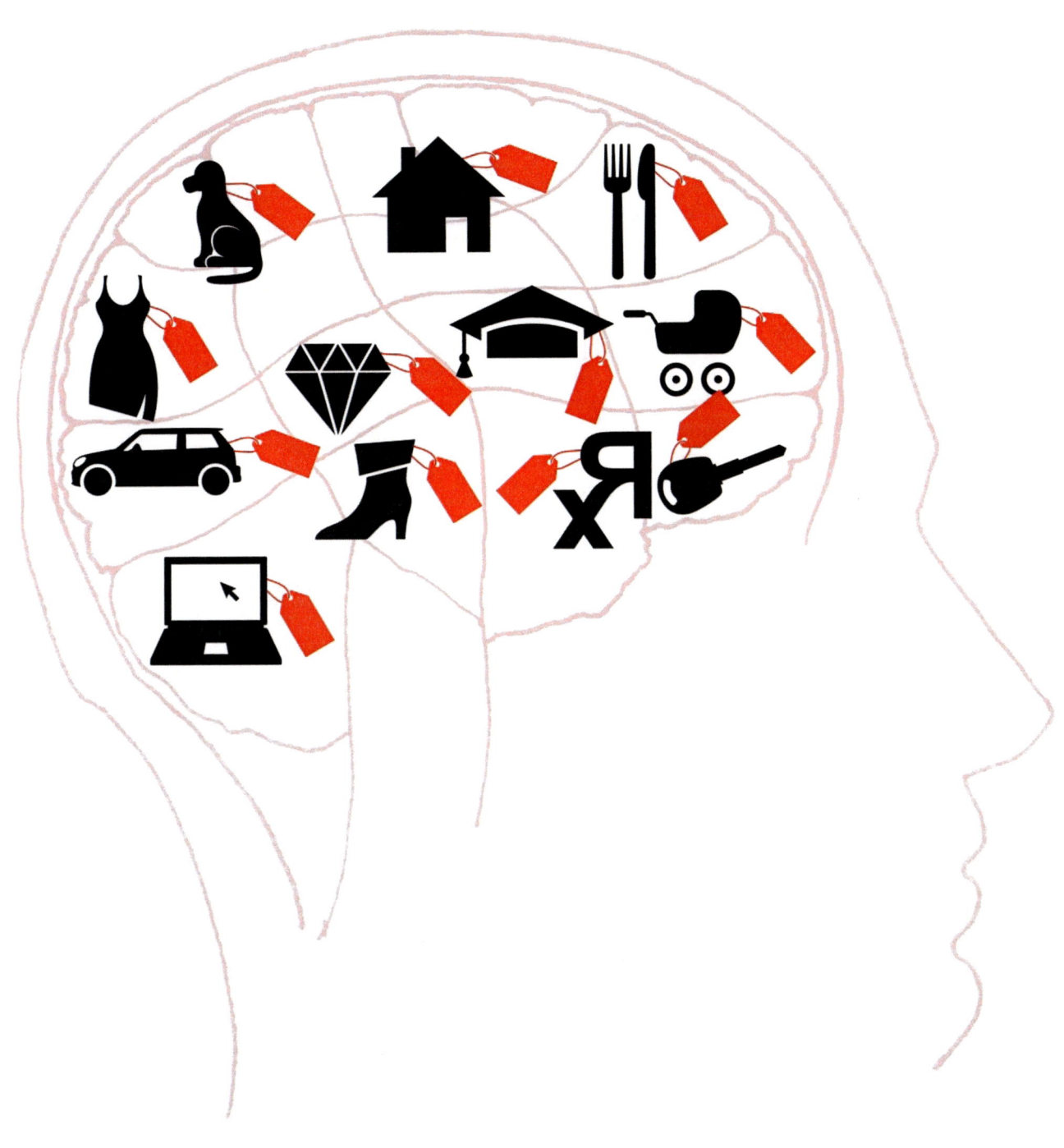

Scents of Success

There are so many ways to apply the art and science of branding; once you know and understand the principles behind the work we are talking about, really the sky is the limit. In this final section, I bring you a few more real-life examples, plus some of the current work-in-progress, along with a handful of invaluable tools, including a table at the end of book you can remove for reference without reducing the contents of the book.

Enjoy!

Revelers celebrate Graduation at Queen's University, produced by the Author.

A Background in Branding

Up in Smoke

June 2001: It was a mid-afternoon flight, most of the way across the country. My seatmate, Lulu Vibert, former model, chatelaine, 'hostess with the mostess', and current event director for Benson and Hedges was taciturn. I tried, with little success, to engage her in conversation. As we would be working together closely for the next three days in Edmonton, city of my birth, I thought it would be wise to get comfortable now. But I had the sinking feeling she would be more comfortable if my business partner Trevor, was there. He was the more extravert, life of the party, type.

This was the fourth major city on our cross-country tour. My company was producing nightclub events with Lulu on a touring 'jet to Ibiza' theme. The gimmick was the nightclub was decked out, usually on a Friday or Saturday night, with Benson and Hedges gimcrack. The props were pretty extensive, and included a replica of the interior of an airplane fuselage we set up in the entryway, through which everyone had to enter the club space.

Faux 'stewardesses' (they were not 'flight attendants') in custom gold lame mini dresses and high-top boots welcomed partiers. Inside the club, enormous palm treetops hung from the ceiling, backlit gold Venetian masks and various other props decorated the space. Although smoking had not been legal inside clubs for a couple of years, cigarette companies were still permitted to sponsor nightclub events and boy did they ever!

A video crew and closed-circuit screens caught one lucky couple each night at each event on camera as they were awarded the 'jet to Ibiza' grand prize. At the end of the summer, Benson and Hedges chartered a jet and sent all the winners on an all-expense paid vacation to the hedonistic playground of Ibiza.

The median age of our audience was about 21, maybe 22. (In most of Canada the drinking age was, and still is 19.) I knew, from meetings at Benson and Hedges, that this was their 'sweet spot'. If they could convince young adults to try their product—even just a little, the statistical chance of hooking them on it 'for life' (hahaha) was relatively high—if it was cross-associated with something, fun, glamorous, 'adult'—like going to Ibiza. The threshold? Just 9 cigarettes a week. They just needed them to smoke those 9 cigarettes…

I don't know how many young adults we helped convince to smoke that summer. I do know, that at the Benson and Hedges boardroom, only 2 or 3 of the 14 or so executives around the table were smokers.

There was no need to prove anything. No sales conversations ever took place. No logical arguments were ever provided (or if they were, at the insistence of the brand sponsor, that is when people tuned off). Branding is pure emotion and it can sell anything. After one summer of peddling cigarettes to teenagers (this was before cigarette promotion was banned in Canada), when I turned in my airline seat to my business associate, who held the contract for national promotions and asked her, "What do you think of what we are doing?" Her response, typically candid, was "I don't think about it, dear."

That, however, made me think: I could no longer 'not think' about the fact that we were systematically providing sponsorship and promotion of a highly addictive and painfully lethal product to young, impressionable kids. (In Canada, the legal drinking age in most provinces is 19). So, I quit.

I stopped doing the circuit, stopped promoting, in fact I almost stopped working altogether. It was just too depressing. Was all I was put here to do promote a heinous corporate agenda through my God-given creative talents and effort? Surely, there had to be more to it.

By this time I had developed such a strong intuition for branding and promotions I could see before the fact whether national and international marketing campaigns would succeed—or most likely—fail: most campaigns and most brands DO fail—this is one of the truisms of the world of brands and I wondered why it is that brands and campaigns that were doomed to fail had millions of dollars and thousands of hours of human capital invested in them. There had to be a reason. It was obvious to me—didn't anyone else notice?

As it turns out, no one (much) else did. Intuition is a curious thing. It emerges slowly, like the stars on a clear night at dusk, and then brightens until not much else is visible. And recent brain research suggests that it isn't all psychic babble either. Intuition has very good reason for working—it is based on real-life experience. By opening myself to an enormous breadth and range of business and marketing experience I had been able to develop a 'sixth sense' for brand marketing that correctly predicted, with uncanny accuracy, what would work, and what didn't.

Yet, there remained one problem: how could I help others see what I saw?

So began my mission, to codify and backtrack my 'intuitive' knowledge into linear, sound logic that anyone with the interest and sufficient dedication could learn and apply. My target? The people who own, run and manage the millions of smaller sized businesses about the world. The people who didn't have Madison Avenue, and Wall Street backing their efforts. The people who had genuine missions and have not become so cynical that all they see is money lining their closets. Everyday people, like my many clients over the years with good ideas, better ideas and no way to compete with the billion-dollar war chests of the multinationals. But wait! Those billion-dollar war chests were being spent on all sorts and kinds of brands and marketing that failed! The big guys are playing a craps game, with so much money to spend, they don't mind losing a few million, here and there. I wanted to benefit the guys without millions to spare, but who really had a care.

I knew doing this was risky. For instance, what if the big guys got a hold of this first? Would they use this information to do away with their flops and run successful campaigns 100% of the time? What if branding was seen as too esoteric by the average guy? In truth, these fears may have had their place at one time, but the world now is different than it was twenty years ago when I began this project. Multinationals are running a lot leaner today, and scrambling for market share in a rapidly changing knowledge economy which has values that shift seemingly overnight. For another, the average small business owner, at least in North America was increasingly savvy. While some people still ask me 'what is branding?', most people now understand that what I do has nothing (or little) to do with a hot iron applied to flesh or fur.

The time to let the cat out of the bag was here. It is time for this book.

And I knew by the end of the summer that while I was doing exactly the work I had set out to do ten years before, I was done with it. I now knew the power of Brands was so powerful, precise and exacting, it could successfully peddle poison to people. I now knew exactly how.

I also knew it was time to switch clients.

It has taken me many years to discover this was not just a change of clients, but a change in values, in myself. After over twelve years of gestation, this became a driving force to document the core elements explained in this book, so that entrepreneurs (with all their great twenty-first century ideas) can use these methods, which helps level the playing field!

The MarkBrand method, developed by the Author, is a process map effective in branding from the inside out. It.is an open architecture system that models all project components to singular stable process map, outlined below:

NAME SUBSTANCE **SHARE ACTION**

CREATES DEVELOPS
STRATEGY DESIGN

STRATEGY & DEVELOPMENT   **CREATIVE & DESIGN**

$ i

RELATIONSHIPS & PROJ. MNGMNT.   **RESEARCH & ANALYSIS**

BUILDS ADAPTS TO
SALES MARKET

BUILD RESULTS   **EXPRESS CATALYST**

Branding as a Profession

Like many children, as a very small child, I had one and sometimes two very close relationships. The relationships we have with our parents, as infants, go on to create our view of the world, and of ourselves. Our mother comes to represent all that is warm, intuitive, kind and loving. Our father represents safety, security and authority. Most parents do their very best to fulfill these roles, and regardless of the sometimes-complicated relationships we have with our parents, if you are reading this book; it is likely you had individuals who filled these roles. What do these common-to-almost-all human relationships demonstrate? Simply this: **emotion** and **rationality**. Regardless of your gender, your first, primordial experience— and life-giving relationship was with mother, while rationality was frequently passed on through dear old dad. While not exclusively true (and if yours was opposite, so be it) these forms are considered standards of behavior sufficient to become archetypes—that is to say, primal forms throughout humanity.

Carl Jung, the famous twentieth century trail-blazing psychologist, developed the concepts of archetype in psychology, demonstrating that for most people these and other 'standard forms' of relationship, emotions and rationality were if not entirely explicit, then certainly implicit through dreams, meditation or hypnosis. Jung went even further, distinguishing how these archetypes operate on powerful, civilization-wide meta signals that inform and corroborate, defining 'normal' behaviors, expectations and produce these self-same 'roles', like mother and father; not to mention 'good daughter', 'loose woman', 'eldest son', and 'prodigal'. All of these roles (and more) will be important to know and understand in grasping just how brands, and branding truly works.

Just as there actually is no 'ideal family' (fortunately, we left behind that concept with television's Cleavers in the 1950s) there actually is no one 'best' form or branding for all situations. However, what we do have are effective and proven working models (just as we may have in child-rearing).

The 'ideal' brand is like an 'ideal' human. Relatable, dependable, attractive and intelligent—but just right, not 'too much'. Should your brand be pretty and popular, like the cheerleader of your high school, or athletic and driven, like the all-star jock? Could be either, or neither—never both. These popular archetypes are indeed executable brand archetypes, but there are others that may or may not be equally or more appropriate to your enterprise.

Archetype assists with developing brand identity

Most people are born knowing what gender they are, and where they fit in the family unit. They are either eldest son, or second daughter, or what-have-you. Such categories are highly informing of human dynamics and all relationships. One study noted that two children from different continents, races and languages have more in common with each other if they share the same birth order (i.e. first, middle, last) than their own siblings, in their own families. This is due to the fact that context is all-decisive. Did you know that last children tend to be the fastest walkers? The reason—they learned how to walk quickly in order to keep up with the rest of their family unit. The eldest sets the pace, the youngest keep up. As the youngest grows up, they retain the longer stride they learned as youngsters.

Brands, unlike people, aren't born with the clarity of understanding their 'place.' Being synthetic creations; they need us, using our rational minds, to identify their gender and place. When this is done expertly and explicitly the results are amazing. I discovered that branding may contribute up to 60%—*or more*—to a company's balance sheet! Correctly leveraged and utilized, this tool is an indispensable aid in communications, employee resolve and planning company direction and vision; not to mention sales and marketing.

Branding as a field

Branding is a 'narrow but wide' field or niche in business and consulting. It is narrow because it confines itself to communications and it is wide because it concerns itself at every level of commerce and across all cases.

Brand managers are the normal representatives of branding. These managers are usually employed by larger companies to oversee a specific brand (or brands). Typically, they specialize in the understanding of the inner workings of a specific brand, including both its gestalt—the feeling around it through its people, and the operational requirements of the corporation, which owns it. Brand managers tend to be good project managers as well as having a good creative 'sense' of what fits and what does not with their company's brand.

Brand architects, such as myself, are fewer in number, partly because as of this date there is not a single graduate program in branding taught in American universities (check data:). Typically, like myself, brand architects stumble onto their career following a diverse career in business, including various facets like marketing, sales and human resource management in a variety of industries and at various levels of both management and scale of business. This peripatetic work history provides the necessary background for us to see the overreaching patterns that work beyond the specific data and experiences provided by any one company or industry.

Brand architects work to create and establish brands from the ground up, including developing company cultures that support the resonance of a brand. A typical brand architect is a visionary CEO (think Steve Jobs or Steve Ballmer). A few brand architects work independently as co-creative consultants to CEOs. The advantage of an external brand architect is the same as having an external architect—external perspectives tend to provide more objective and 'out of the box' thinking than a single internal resource, while also being freed from the exigencies of day-to-day management and direction of an organization to focus solely on brand strategy.

Meaningful work as a branding professional

My own experience as a branding specialist, and eventually a brand architect, came about gradually through a varied career path. In a like manner, the concept of *Signs & Symbols of Success* dawned gradually, sometime after my first fifteen years and 150 different client brand experiences. Through these experiences I slowly began to see patterns that allowed me to begin to predict what 'works' and what 'will never work' in a particular market scenario. Slowly, it dawned on me that there was no special brilliance or creative intelligence that was being applied by my mind—rather, my mind has formed sets of 'behavior rules' that allowed it to begin seeing quickly what fit—and what did not, in scenario after scenario. I began to see bankruptcies and strategic errors of large and small brands before they occurred. And, I could correctly predict when a new or emerging brand hit all the right notes and would succeed beyond even the dreams of its owner(s).

Over the next ten or so years I painstakingly worked backwards through my own mind to unravel the patterns that had been laid, that allowed my brain to see these things almost instantaneously. The result was The Unspoken Promise: the realization that very few brands (if any) succeed without resonating their entire 'being', including packaging, communications, price, offer and internal corporate culture around a single high-level promise, which is not only unspoken, but most often virtually invisible to everyone involved—and yet, which nevertheless is quite real and impacts everything (think of gravity, if you are wondering what a parallel concept might be). Like gravity, everyone knows about the unspoken promise, but takes it so much for granted that no conversation is required to communicate its effects or impact.

In my study of the global 100—the top 100 brands, documented annually in the Interbrand 100, I have seen that not only does every successful brand conform resolutely and holistically throughout its organization to a single unspoken promise—but also that no one promise is 'owned' exclusively one brand. In fact, all proved brands conform to but one of only seven 'types'. Because there are so few proven, successful formulas for branding, my brain had been able to spot the differences and could quickly see what was going on in any situation. It really was an extraordinary day when I realized how few are the routes to branding success!

Learning about brands and branding came for me, organically. As there are not any graduate programs taught in North American universities, this can hardly be unusual. What's different is that I am a self-taught entrepreneur, with a creative background. I studied art, art history and color in college and university. After that I took sales at the local technical institute and moved right into business. To me, the point of education is application, and I didn't see any further studying to be of added use or value at the time.

When desktop computers developed the ability to produce 'desktop publishing' I became one of the first power users of the new software and laser printers, producing books, manuscripts, recipes, manuals, and resumes for a varied downtown clientele. Eventually, I moved onto pure graphics, such as logos, brand materials, brochures, signage and later, storefront design, window design and merchandising. Throughout my interest was in developing understanding of what made it all work.

After several years of co-owning a highly successful visual merchandising company in Vancouver Canada, with dozens of top retail clients, including Chanel, Timberland and many other local and national retailers with outlets in Vancouver I moved to Toronto, Canada's largest city to pursue further understanding of brands and branding. This sojourn developed into becoming an event designer and producer.

Through the lights, camera action of events I soon saw that the capacity to communicate emotionally was primary. And through events, emotions could be generated instantaneously. Literally in one moment: a person was outside of an event, about to pass through a doorway, and then, boom: they entered into another world, a world of color, action, suspended belief and even fantasy. You could see it on their faces. Linking events to corporate promotion became my modus, and the ability to link the event to the mission or mood of the corporation's brand was my mission. After about two hundred such events I came to realize I could create literally any emotion, at will. And through my events, people became brand ambassadors, without any need to sign up for anything.

Lest you begin to think that all this work is only in quest of corporate work, check out the chart at right, developed at Government Efficiency.

To the right is an extract from the concluding report I generated from the Government events. This report became the foundation of what is now the Alberta Public Service values, guiding the day to day policy of over 30,000 public sector employees.

Below is some of artwork developed for the PEAK process roles, another product inspired by the MarkBrand method.

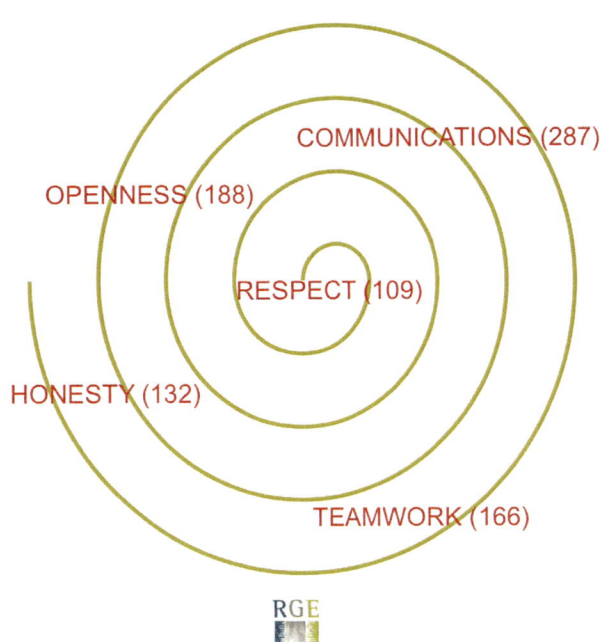

VALUES
THE 5 VALUES MENTIONED MOST FREQUENTLY BY STAFF IN BETTER TOGETHER I, II, III, IV.

COMMUNICATIONS (287)

OPENNESS (188)

RESPECT (109)

HONESTY (132)

TEAMWORK (166)

RGE

Getting Media Ready in Shifting Sands

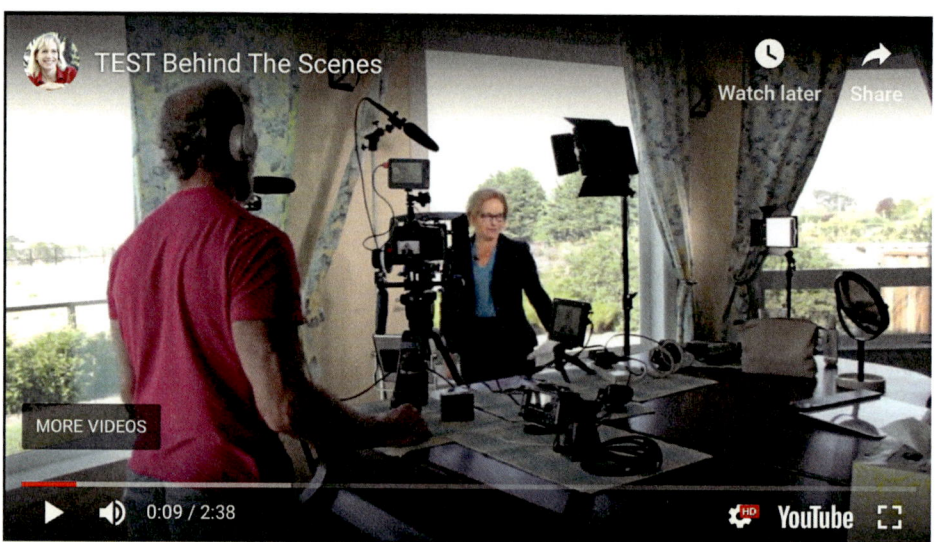

The author in the foreground, working with sister Aurora Winter, in California.

By now, if you have not noticed the dramatically shifting nature of media, you have clearly been living under a rock for a while or have been off-world on a vacation to Venus.

More than ever, media preparedness is a prerequisite to success. Understanding how media works, what's in it for you, and how to connect through media has always been a moving puzzle-piece. Today's shifting sands require spontaneity along with preparedness to the highest degree, in order to realize brand success.

With over thirty years of experience in branding it is fair to say that the last decade—overlapping the introduction of the iPhone—has been the most revolutionary. While the classic principles still apply, the tactical means employed are changing minute to moment.

Handling all the changes in media, means you are riding a wave of adapting and changing digital platforms with rules and systems that are in flux.

Spotlight: Focus Your Strengths

How interested are you in success?

While the bar is high, so are the rewards. Today, in the distracted years of the late teens of the twenty-first century it is possible to upset apple carts, overcome lifetime bans or separations, create new contacts plus rapidly share, receive and respond to messages. The fact that it is theoretically possible to also do so at a scale previously unimagined means there has NEVER been greater opportunity, nor demand.

I have found the best way to ensure you get to the top of your game is to write down some notes. I've designed a few here to target your thinking about your brand. You will find this helpful if you want to shift the direction you are heading or just want to improve.

Think about your strengths, what sparks joy?

Whether you are out to change the world or change a window display, branding is both a practical and valuable lens through which to view the world. To benefit more from branding, these questions will kick off a process that is designed to help you see beyond your blind spots into opportunity!

Brand realization impact survey (for your brand):

1   Estimated impact of the current rate of growth in your industry.
     (What's going on locally, globally, environmentally, politically...)

_____

_____

_____

_____

_____

_____

2   When do you think is the time interval for improvement?
    What is the change cycle? A year? A decade? A month? Why?

    _____

    _____

    _____

    _____

    _____

3   What's the likely next, no matter what?
    What's the almost probable, almost certain future, stated as a problem?

    _____

    _____

    _____

    _____

    _____

    _____

    _____

4   What's needed?

    _____

    _____

    _____

    _____

    _____

    _____

5   What's new? *What's happening in your business area or with your clientele?*

_____

_____

_____

_____

6   What's going on in your industry?
What's going on in general and specifically with competition?

_____

_____

_____

7   What's possible?

_____

_____

_____

8   What's at stake?

_____

_____

_____

9   What will happen with status quo?

_____

_____

_____

10   What could happen with improvement?

_____

_____

_____

_____

11   What else? *If the above are accomplished, what will be the consequences.*

_____

_____

_____

_____

12   What would a miracle look like?

_____

_____

_____

13   What is next?

_____

_____

_____

_____

_____

_____

What does branding work look like?

Branding is exciting work—particularly when approached from the perspective of designing experience and connection. This is how I approach it.

While Branding work occurs in real-time and space, here is what we can show in a book. Work in process can look like any of the photos and designs here.

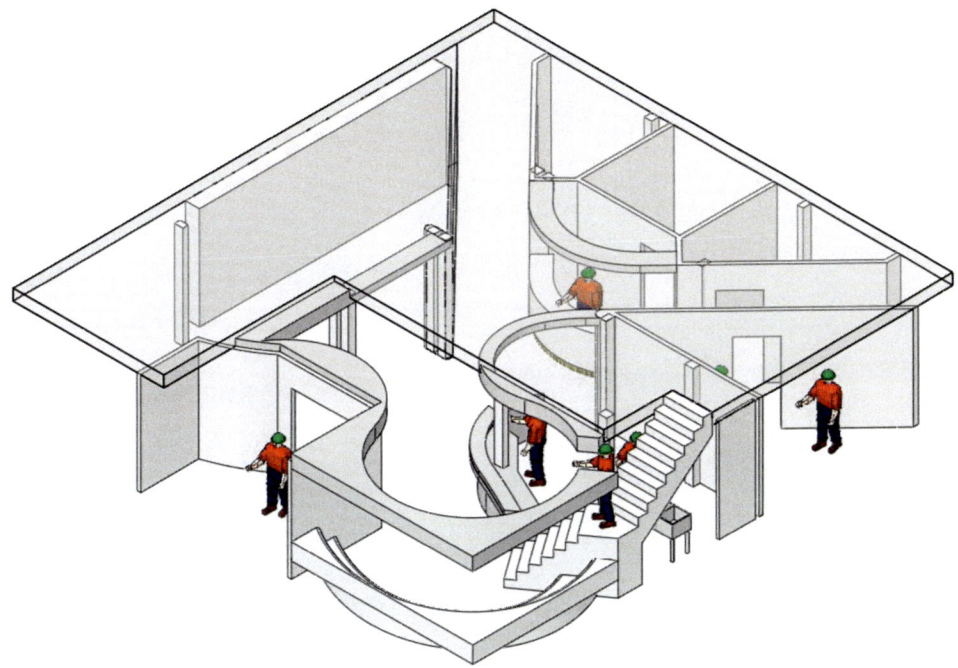

Store layout and traffic design for new gym, above.

One of the color-ways, below.

COLORWAY #4: ALIVE

DESCRIPTION: A clean contemporary palette with bright primaries and vibrant, energetic complementary contrasts toned down with Asian wood tones and a cool Silver Gray

A suite of coupon certificate exchange voucher designs, and event execution, below.

Cross-brain associations caused by selection of words and standardized colors, below. From left to right: Concept, color group(s), chromatic order, Name, PMS reference.

CROMA Chromatic Residual Optimized Marketing Architectonics

16 COLORS FUELING THE PROMISE OF HARDCORE BRANDS

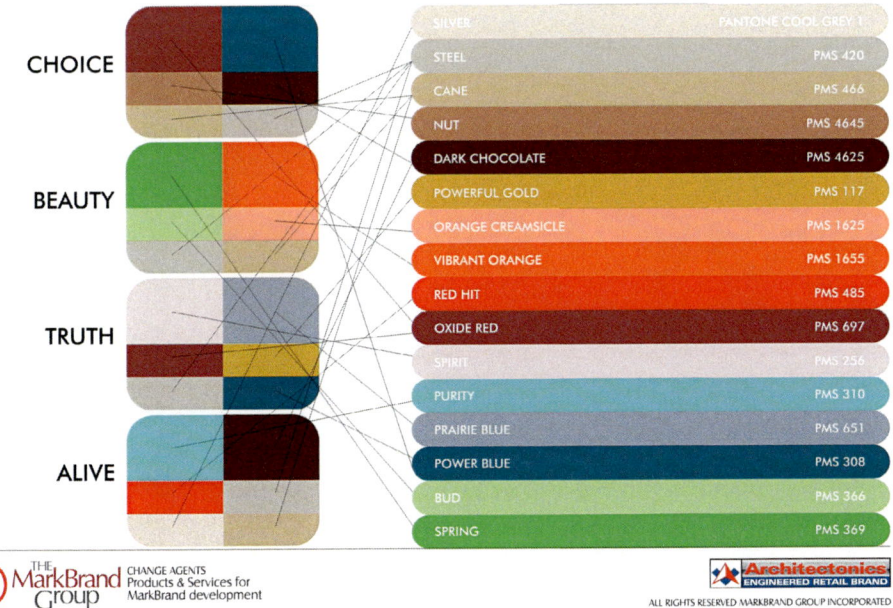

CHOICE		SILVER	PANTONE COOL GREY 1
		STEEL	PMS 420
		CANE	PMS 466
		NUT	PMS 4645
BEAUTY		DARK CHOCOLATE	PMS 4625
		POWERFUL GOLD	PMS 117
		ORANGE CREAMSICLE	PMS 1625
		VIBRANT ORANGE	PMS 1655
TRUTH		RED HIT	PMS 485
		OXIDE RED	PMS 697
		SPIRIT	PMS 256
		PURITY	PMS 310
ALIVE		PRAIRIE BLUE	PMS 651
		POWER BLUE	PMS 308
		BUD	PMS 366
		SPRING	PMS 369

BRYCE MAYNARD WINTER

Personal Brand built by the Author on year away, below:

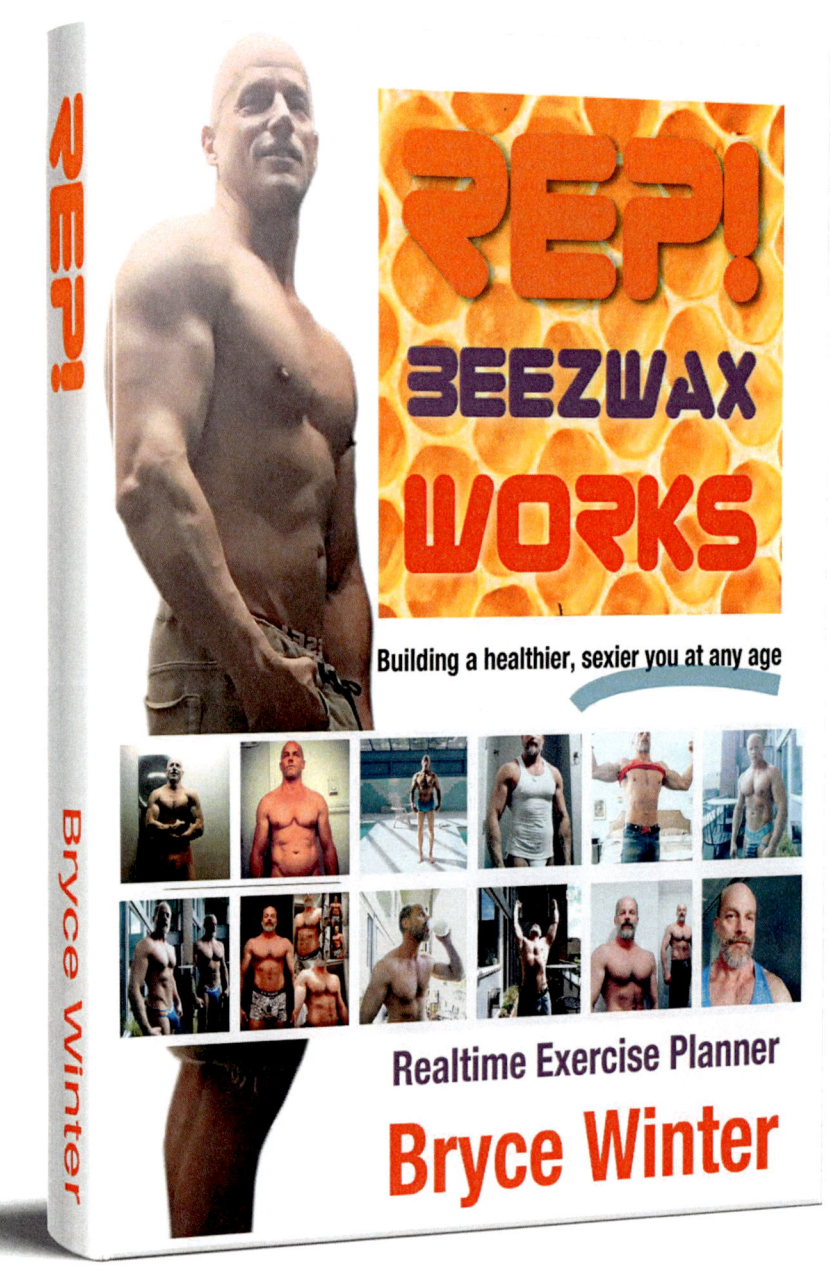

https://instagram.com/brandbryce/
https://beezwax.works

Catalog Cover design for and iconography for PEAK thinking types collateral.

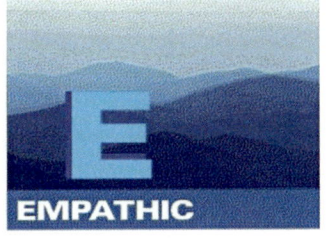

The Explorer Suite

For years I have been sifting and sorting what I consider to be the points of highest leverage and greatest intrinsic interest to explore, relating to the world of branding. Today, I have a strong awareness that more than ever we must 'swim' with the currents, even while we prepare for new levels of interactive media coming. With media evolving it is time for a new kind of brand that embraces technology. I call this GENR8 (pronounced just like *generate*).

If you would like to get right to work in learning and applying some of these latest concepts in the newest technology and most cutting-edge technology, then I invite you to learn more about these initiatives.

- MONDEX8
- The Media Lab
- GENR8 ELEV8R

MONDEX8

The World Needs You!

MONDEX8 is designed for the active integration of communication between people and machines. It is an ACTIVE INTERFACE LANGUAGE that may compete in the all-in-one sweepstakes, including currency. The application of MONDEX8 is the topic of an upcoming book; and inclues: facebook.com/mondex8/

THE MEDIA LAB

The Media Lab is our new-for-2019 real time branding venture designed to bring creative forces together to produce effective branding with live events. This book is the first of many products of The Media Lab. TheMediaLab.space

GENR8 ELEV8R

The GENR8 ELEV8R is active interface technology with BIOMIMETIC AI. It takes advantage of MONDEX8 to apply it to smartphone mobile technology to create a totally new, seamless experience designed the way you think. Learn more and connect at facebook.com/genr8me/

❶ The Media Lab

Casecode 'ten-thirteen'   0311-1004-1013

Outcome Media Development Licensing System for Business

- What if there was a turnkey licensing system for entrepreneurs?
- What if didn't need to worry about systems or structure?
- What if you and could just *get right to work*?

Opportunity We are offering CLIENTS and DEVELOPERS the opportunity to become ground-floor partners in a new real time market branding system that is uniquely inclusive, and profitable.

Core aspects There are two distinct aspects to The Media Lab. 1) The ability to develop systems and structure to a critical, core baseline of global expectations, ensuring all aspects of the business are present and function according to the market's needs. 2) A centralized ability to advertise and sell branded products and services.

Components Some of the key components of the The Media Lab system include Event Modelling, Human Resource Development, Tactical and Strategic Design Market Messaging as well as a distinct Membership Sales System.

TheMediaLab.space

❷ GENR8 ELEV8R
X8 active interface technology with BIOMIMETIC AI

GENR8 ELEV8R technology is a sophisticated four-dimensional open-architecture model of human and corporate behavior.

GENR8 Technology Group is creating a new level of connectivity and commitment between partners with the cutting-edge community owned and controlled secure, private artificial intelligence, launching 2020.

GENR8 is unprecedented in business and therefore comparisons are difficult. Therefore, we describe many key attributes and trust the reader to develop understanding.

Eight fundamental elements of the strategy are:

1. Sticky-slippery quality (once you try, you must buy; goes down easy)
2. Finite size with infinite scalability (can start small, grow enormous)
3. Multi-level communications (conscious, unconscious, any and all)
4. Cell-like structures (cohesive, replicable, holographic by nature)
5. Training system (training & coaching integral components)
6. Universality (systems apply anywhere, anytime)
7. Leverage (getting a lot of result for a little effort)
8. Breakthroughs (unprecedented results)

The product and corporate strategy are built using these criteria.

Meta labels (below) are an intrinsic aspect of ELEV8R,
giving it an immersive, active, 'push-button' quality.

facebook.com/genr8.elev8r/

About the Author

Bryce Maynard Winter is a Vancouver-based global brand agent obsessed with all things brands including color, human-technical systems and digital communications.

Brand Architect Winter understands what makes people think and what prompts them to action. Combining merchandising and event experience with brands like CHANEL, Evian and TD while coaching identity progression training with creative teams has produced extraordinary results on many levels.

Winter has been distilling archetype theory for decades, using his real-world experience working in +store design, systems design, human resources systems and with branding. His proven, practical strategies produce remarkable results. Today, he is busy building on the systems expounded in this book, developed in 30 years of experience on the front lines with hundreds of client brands.

Winter is a lifelong entrepreneur who connects on a number of topics in ways that entertain, provoke thought and enlighten attitudes. He has produced award-winning creative work promoting global brands such as Aveda, Timberland and Virgin—learning key secrets of branding in the process.

Bryce Maynard Winter is a strategist, educator, coach, trainer and writer who has worked with numerous brands at all levels from strategic to tactical. *Signs & Symbols of Success* is his first book. He is currently working on several more, including an introduction to *MONDEX8*. He lives in Vancouver, Canada.

The Matriarchy of Brands

Thanks for reading, pleasant reader: I hope to hear from you soon.

Keep the chart following in your book and feel free to remove the extra page behind as a desktop, fridge-side or other handy reference chart.

Make sure you register online to obtain the full online resource set, including PDF files you can print or display for yourself at any size.

Get your free bonus materials! Register online today at TheMediaLab.space

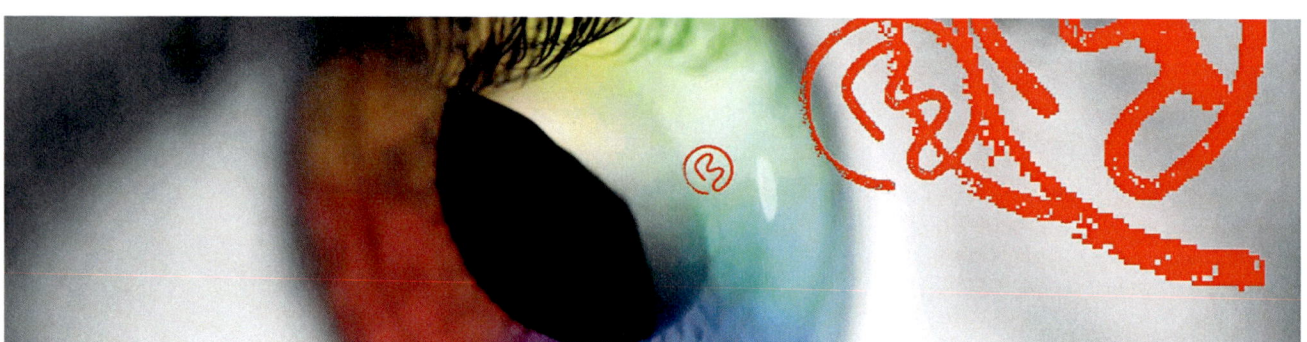

TheMediaLab.space
success@GENR8.me

		THE MATRIARCHY OF BRANDS	HOUSE	TOWER	BRIDGE	HOTEL	CASTLE	PALACE	THEATER
I	Conscious / Color	Hue	Red + Yellow	Green	Blue + Gold, or Orange	Contrast Pair	Blue	Red	Rainbow
II	Failsafe / Form	Shape	Curvaceous, feminine	VIRGINAL	Masculine, modern	Hipster vibe du jour	RECTANGULAR	Anthropomorphic	Anthropomorphic
III	Curious / Question	Brand	What do you want?	Who do you think you are?	Why not you?	Which way R U going?	Where are you going?	When?	How?
IIII	Alternative / Answer	Elevator	What you need	Popularity	Safe Adventure	Choice	Security	Permanence	Inclusion
V	Archetypal / Archetype	Persona	Working Woman Eldest Daughter	Princess Youngest Daughter	Knight Eldest Son	Concierge Youngest Son	King Father	Queen Mother	Theatrical Co. Family
VI	Successful / Scent	Truth	SALTY	MOIST	SWEATY	TOO COOL FOR SCHOOL	SAVORY	SWEET	HOT BUTTER
VII	Perfect / Promise	Secret	More for Less	You, only better	Change of state	Transformation	Safety	Forever	Together
VIII	Trustworthy / Texture	Architecture	House	Tower	Bridge	Hotel	Castle	Palace	Theater
	OLD SCHOOL	CAPS = ALIGNED	whirlpool DENNY'S	BARBIE BODYSHOP	HONDA HARLEY CHEVROLET	general motors	FORD MERCEDES-B.	safeway ROLLS-ROYCE	3M POST-IT
	NEW SCHOOL	lowercase = OFFCODE	MCDONALD'S	STARBUCKS	WALMART/HOME DEPOT	PEPSICO	IBM	COCA-COLA	DISNEY microsoft
			WWW	WHOLE FOODS	AMAZON	TWITTER	FACEBOOK	APPLE	GOOGLE
				LYFT	WEWORK	AIRBNB	TESLA	NETFLIX	YAHOO

CROMA

Chromatic Residual Optimized Marketing Architectonics

MARKKO

Monetized Achievement Residual Key Knowledge Optimization

PERSEUS

Personally Emotive Reciprocal Spirit Express Universal Solution

CRONOS

Chronological Reciprocal Organized Nominal Ordered System

SIGNS & SYMBOLS OF SUCCESS